studies who know little about theology, and for students of theology
who know little about queer studies. Along the way he also provides
critical direction, steering the reader towards new ways of engaging
queer religious texts, and of thinking about queer religious lives, in
contemporary global Christian contexts.'

eeds, UK

61 190 365

QUEER THEOLOGIES

Queer Theologies: The Basics is a concise and illuminating introduction to the study of this controversial and discursive subject area. This book provides an accessible exploration into the major themes within queer studies, queer theologies, and themes of gender and sexuality in Christianity. Topics covered include:

- The development of queer theologies
- Queering 'traditional' theology
- Queer theologies in global contexts
- Queer Bible
- Queer theologies from queer lives

With a glossary of key terms and suggestions for further reading throughout, this book is an ideal starting point for anyone seeking a full introduction to Christian queer theologies as well as broader themes in theology, gender, and sexuality.

Chris Greenough is Senior Lecturer in Theology and Religion, Edge Hill University, UK.

THE BASICS

For more information about this series, please visit: https://www.routledge.com/The-Basics/book-series/B

QUEER THEOLOGIES

CHRIS GREENOUGH

Routledge
Taylor & Francis Group

LONDON AND NEW YORK

First published 2020
by Routledge
2 Park Square, Milton Park, Abingdon, Oxon OX14 4RN

and by Routledge
52 Vanderbilt Avenue, New York, NY 10017

Routledge is an imprint of the Taylor & Francis Group, an informa business

© 2020 Chris Greenough

British Library Cataloguing-in-Publication Data
A catalogue record for this book is available from the British Library

Library of Congress Cataloging-in-Publication Data
A catalog record has been requested for this book

ISBN: 978-1-138-60418-6 (hbk)
ISBN: 978-1-138-60471-1 (pbk)
ISBN: 978-0-429-46843-8 (ebk)

Typeset in Bembo
by Taylor & Francis Books

CONTENTS

ACKNOWLEDGEMENTS

I am grateful to Rebecca Shillabeer, senior editor at Routledge, for commissioning this book, as well as the support from Jack Boothroyd, editorial assistant. Thanks also to Roger Browning for his diligent work as copy editor.

The time and space afforded to work on this and other projects was supported by Edge Hill University's Research Investment Fund: I thank the RIF Steering Group and the University's Research Office for the provision of such helpful resources. Thanks to Heather Marshall for covering my teaching relief. The arrival into my first academic post at Edge Hill University has been supported by wonderful colleagues and enthusiastic students. I thank the former Dean of the Faculty of Education, Dr Lynnette Turner, for her cheery encouragement and support. My gratitude is also extended to my kind, brilliant colleagues, especially Maggie Webster, Paul Smalley, Sjay Patterson-Craven, Shirley Hindley, Michaela Smith, Dr Cathy Butterworth, Dr Francis Farrell, Dr Damien Shortt, and former Head of Department, Dr Phil Rigby. Thank you to my friends for checking in on me and for listening to musings about the project, especially Becky Fiddler, Helen Thomas, Marie Bennett, Dr Monika Reece, and Dr Sarah Misra.

Endless thanks to friendly, supportive colleagues elsewhere in the academy – particularly Dr Deryn Guest, Prof Andrew Yip, Dr Katie Edwards, Dr Meredith Warren, Dr Caroline Blyth, Dr Adriaan van Klinken, Dr Dawn Llewellyn, Prof Hannah Bacon, and Prof Johanna Stiebert.

Thanks also to my wonderful partner, Dr Mark Edward, who drags me away from the keyboard and makes me laugh daily, as well as my loving and caring family.

Finally, the deepest debt of gratitude I have is for the brave scholars whose work has paved the way for such a guide on queer theologies to be needed. Each and every text referenced in this book has served to fuel me. This book is in honour of these queer saints.

INTRODUCTION

The book is an introductory text, aimed at non-specialists or those coming to the area for the first time. Readers, therefore, may be students, researchers, academics, clergy, laypeople or those with a general interest in the field. Each chapter is designed to stand alone, and this allows immediate access to different themes in order to suit the interests of a wide range of readers. It is important to emphasise that this is a 'basics' book. Condensing the academic field of queer theologies into a beginners' guide is no easy task. This is particularly difficult as a number of texts within queer theory and queer theologies are known for being very challenging in terms of the academic language used. In the hope that the reader will share the same passions and motivations for such an exciting field of study, my intention is to ensure that the language used throughout this text is purposefully accessible. Due to this fact I am acutely aware of significant voices in the scholarship of queer theologies who may be critical that this pursuit of accessibility means the depth of material has been compromised in some way. To address this concern, at the end of each chapter I provide a brief list of suggested further reading and online resources. A comprehensive bibliography for each chapter also lists all the references throughout the discussion and directs readers to further study. Following this basic introduction I urge readers to explore the suggested texts and authors for themselves. In this book I have attempted to give some organisation and structure in the form of chapters and sections, yet structure and order are both *unqueer*. Where themes and structures overlap I have assigned them to the most suitable chapter and heading for discussion. Additionally, a glossary provides working definitions for a number of terms used in the text.

The focus of this book is Christian queer theologies, an area which has garnered much attention in the field of theology and religious studies. Queer theory has become a growing area of critical studies within the academy. Universities are offering courses on gender, sexuality, and queer studies. Such courses may be taught by queer-identifying individuals, while some may not. Queer theory has been applied across academic subjects, such as the arts, humanities, and social sciences. One of my aims with this book is to introduce readers in an accessible way to the authors, themes, histories, movements, and texts which have shaped queer theologies. Of course, all of these ideas are not mine! Therefore, there are a number of academic references throughout.

There is a common practice among feminist and queer writers that they will offer some detail about themselves as part of their writing. This is to provide some context about the author: their location, position, and some aspects of their identity which may be considered important to the text. Following this custom I offer my own position as a cisgender, gay, Christian, queer theologian. Nevertheless, each of these markers of identification – 'cisgender', 'gay', 'Christian', 'queer' – does not accurately represent who I am. They may give some clues, but they leave additional questions. With 'gay', for example, the reader may wonder if I am celibate, married, have a partner? How does being gay coexist with being Christian? The reader may also wonder if I am a practising Christian, or to which denomination I belong. I may have already been thought of as a 'liberal' Christian, given the context of the book. What does a gay, queer Christian look like? There are also aspects of my identification which I did not include, such as those relating to race, dis/ability, class, and so on. In many respects there is an almost failure of each of the adjectives used above to describe me, and this failure is similar to what 'queer' is about. Queer is a term which does not adequately describe those who use it. It is an ambiguous word, which cannot be pinned down satisfactorily.

To give a small taster for the contents of the book, here I offer a very brief sketch of three important questions: (1) what is queer? (2) what is theology? and (3) why is this important?

WHAT IS QUEER?

One of the earlier definitions of 'queer' meant 'strange' or 'odd'. But the term was also later used in the form of homophobic verbal abuse (for further discussion, see Namaste, 1999). This insult was later reclaimed, and was used to describe lesbian, gay, bisexual, transgender, and other individuals who identify as non-normative in terms of their gender or sexuality. 'Non-normative' does not mean 'non-normal'. 'Non-normative' is an important catch-all term used to refer to people whose self-identifications and/or sexualities do not align with traditional and dominant ideas of gender and sex. The traditional understanding of gender has, until very recently, been based on biological sex: male or female. A binary is a system of two opposites. Therefore, the dominant understanding of gender has been determined through the gender binary: either male or female. Similarly, heterosexuality has been privileged as the dominant sexuality.

Thankfully, life in the 21st century has witnessed radical and significant shifts in human understandings of gender and sexualities. Such shifts are down to the work of gender theorists and of activists. Gender theorists saw how traditional views on binary gender (male/female) were restrictive. Important critical thinking in gender studies revealed how biological sex does not automatically determine gender, and that gender is a construct (this will be expanded on in Chapter 1). Therefore, *intersex, transgender, transsexual, non-binary, gender-fluid* and *queer* widen the scope of our understanding of gender. In addition to heterosexuality, *homosexuality, bisexuality, pansexuality, polysexuality, asexuality* are all legitimate forms of sexual identification. See the Glossary for a definition of each of these terms.

The work of gender theorists ran parallel to the work of activists, who wanted to promote equality for all identifications of gender and sexuality. In time, the activist movement led to changes in how we view non-normative identities, particularly in terms of psychology. Previously, for example, to be gay was considered a psychological illness. Moreover, in large parts of the world there have been significant changes in laws which now protect the rights of individuals in relation to their gender and sexuality.

In addition to the definition of 'queer' as 'odd', and as a collective grouping for non-normative identifications of gender/sexuality, there is a third, critical, usage of the word 'queer' which emerges from its use as an academic term. In this context 'queer' means to 'disturb' or 'disrupt'. It is this definition that was later applied to theory, and theology, as a critical lens. It calls for the uncovering and dismantling of power structures. Further discussion on this use of queer is found in Chapter 1.

WHAT IS THEOLOGY?

Theology is a word made up from two Greek compounds: *Theos* (God) and *logos* (word). Theology therefore means 'words about God' or 'speaking of God'. Christian theologians talk about God and use sources such as the Bible, the writings from early saints, Church history, and human reason. Theology also examines human experience of faith and religion, what people believe and how they practise their beliefs, as well as the relationship between their religion to society and culture.

This book offers an accessible pathway into exploring 'queer theologies'. Queer theologies disrupt the tradition of Christianity, including the Bible, and demonstrate how it has treated some groups unfavourably. Queer theologians have re-examined theology and the history of Christian thought, beliefs and practices, and hold the view that it has, in some way, always been queer (for example, Loughlin, 2007). This is further discussed in Chapter 2. At the same time, 'queer' theologies have referenced non-normative gender and sexuality, and this has been one of the major concerns with theologians in the area of study. Evidently, important theologies emerging from LGBTQ+ contexts have had a major impact on its development and on individuals and communities. In this sense, queer theologies are radical as they work for change. They ask important questions, they challenge accepted ideas, and they allow new, more inclusive, theologies to emerge from queer contexts. In many respects, rather than talking about 'queer theology' in the singular, as has often been done by those in the field, it is more appropriate to talk about 'queer theologies' as a plural term. It is misleading to suggest that all queer theologians are talking about the same thing! There is no universal 'queer theology' and queer theologians are rarely neutral in the approaches they adopt.

WHY ARE QUEER THEOLOGIES IMPORTANT?

Queer theologies examine how Christianity has been constructed throughout history and ask questions about what voices and experiences have been excluded. This destabilises the structures of power which have been tied up in the religion. Theology is tied up with power, as there are authority structures within church organisations that have developed teachings or biblical interpretations which have had enormous influence in society and culture. Queer theologies interrogate this power.

In some parts of the world, to identify publicly as non-normative is a criminal offence and can be punishable by death. To cite the example of sexuality, data from the International Lesbian, Gay, Bisexual, Trans and Intersex Association (ILGA)[1] in 2019 reveal 70 countries which upheld laws against homosexuality. A further 55 countries neither protect individuals against discrimination based on their sexual orientation, nor do they criminalise consensual same-sex acts between adults. Penalties exist from imprisonment to death. Religion is often used as a justification to discriminate against those who identify as non-normative within these contexts. So there is much-needed work to be done on an activist level to continue to fight against prejudice and injustice. It is also significant to note that while protection by law exists in a number of countries, this does not eradicate homophobic or transphobic attacks of discrimination.

Contextual theologians examine particular communities and experiences – contexts – to shape talk about God. Contextual theologies include feminist theology, Black theology, Asian American theology, liberation theology, disability theology, and LGBTQ+ theology to name just a few representative examples. In Chapter 3, I examine queer theologies in global contexts. The Bible has also been used to attempt to justify religious positions which are against inclusion of non-normative gender and sexuality. Chapter 4 looks more specifically at the so-called 'texts of terror' in the Bible.

Church organisations have often been thought of as hostile to non-normative individuals, and this is reflected in the positional statements from church organisations about LGBTQ+ people. This is discussed more in Chapter 5. It is hoped that engagement with living experiences of queer identified people will allow others to learn, to empathise, and to effect change – whether on an individual or an institutional level. Queer theologies push boundaries. The relevance and impact of queer theologies for contemporary Christianity, therefore, raise questions and disturb long-held ideas in relation to debates on homosexuality, transgender, what constitutes marriage, ideas of 'family'. Just as the insult 'queer' was reclaimed, there are many individuals who have experienced hostility or rejection from their churches and turned away from faith. Queer theologies remind them of the radical love which must be central to Christianity (Cheng, 2011). Queer theologies matter on a personal and individual level.

QUEER RELIGIOUS LITERACY

There can be an unease around the term 'queer' or when engaging in discussions of gender and sexuality. The language surrounding gender or sexual identification can often be perplexing, especially as the LGBTQ+ acronym continues to grow; for example, LGBTQIAA (lesbian, gay, bisexual, transgender, queer/questioning, intersex, asexual, ally).[2] Where there is a lack of understanding or a fear of making mistakes and upsetting others, people can shy away from important discussions and conversations. Or, where conversations do take place, they may be heated or based on misguided assumptions. This is why it is important to be 'literate' when engaging with queer studies. Queer literacy in this regard does not simply mean knowing each of the terms for gender and sexual identity, but means having the capacity and openness to engage and learn more (Edward & Greenough, 2019).

The idea of queer literacy can be coupled with the idea of religious literacy. Adam Dinham and Matthew Francis advocate a promotion of 'religious literacy' which serves to 'move religion away from anxiety and tension and look at it instead as something far too pervasive, far too interesting, and far too nuanced to write off as too risky to talk about' (Dinham & Francis, 2016: 3). For Dinham and Francis, religious literacy takes the heat out of controversial topics and seeks to shed more light on such issues.

Religion is relevant as it pervades all aspects of society, settings, and sectors, irrespective of an individual's personal beliefs. More significantly, Dinham and Francis highlight its importance on a personal, practical level, stating how religious literacy allows for 'deeper and richer relationships between people involved – deeper understanding of each other's positions and practices of argument' (2016: 45). This is an essential element when engaging with queer theologies.

Engaging in religious literacy does not require an individual to be religious, nor does it aim to promote religion in public life. It allows people (religious or non-religious) to engage in informed conversations with confidence, especially when some of the issues may appear to be controversial. Queer religious literacy tackles such issues head on, and rather than focusing on traditional theology it recognises that there is no common fixed representation of the identities 'Christian' or 'queer'. Engaging with non-normative lives demonstrates how religion is significant on an individual level, rather than on an institutional level.

NOTES

1 See https://ilga.org/maps-sexual-orientation-laws. Information is regularly updated
2 Throughout I use the acronym LGBTQ+

REFERENCES

Cheng, P. S. (2011) *Radical Love: An Introduction to Queer Theology*. New York: Seabury Books.

Dinham, A. and Francis, M. (2016) *Religious Literacy in Policy and Practice*. Bristol: Policy Press.

Edward, M. and Greenough, C. (2019) 'Opening Closets: Visibility, Representation and LGBT+ Research Ethics', in Iphofen, R. (Ed.) *Handbook of Research Ethics and Scientific Integrity*. London: Springer [online first].

Loughlin, G. (Ed.) (2007) *Queer Theology: Rethinking the Western Body*. London: Blackwell.

Namaste, V. K. (1999) The use and abuse of queer tropes: Metaphor and catachresls in queer theory and politics. *Social Semiotics*, 9(2), pp. 213–234.

THE DEVELOPMENT OF QUEER THEOLOGIES

This chapter traces, briefly and in broad strokes, the development of queer theologies, which chronologically followed on from modern liberation theologies and queer theory. The German theologian and philosopher Friedrich Schleiermacher (1768–1834) built on the philosophical principles of Immanuel Kant (1724–1804), and he used them to argue that human understanding of theology and religion is linked to individual experience. This chapter looks at insights from three major theological movements in the development of queer theologies: liberation theology, feminist theology, and lesbian and gay theologies. There are overlaps between each movement not only in terms of the time frames in which they were developed but in the fact that each movement was mobilised by activism in the pursuit of social justice. Before queer theologies came to be known as such, liberation theology and feminist theology were concerned with issues around equality, justice, and inclusion. From the late 1960s, gay and lesbian activism highlighted and responded to injustice and mistreatment from authorities towards non-heterosexual people. At a similar time, early gay and lesbian theologies began to emerge. They reflected on the liberation movement and sought to find an inclusive space within Christianity for lesbian and gay people. In the 1990s the term 'queer theory' was coined, informed by feminist, womanist, and postmodern thought. This chapter therefore provides a brief overview of the rise and agenda of those who came to be known as queer theorists, and the function of queer theory. Insights from these areas provided fertile ground from which queer theologies began to flourish. In offering a brief overview of the predecessors and rise of queer theologies, there is not enough space to give a more detailed narrative than the one traced below. Readers should be drawn to the suggestions for further reading at the end of this chapter in order to plug some of the omissions.

LIBERATION THEOLOGY

Liberation theology developed in Latin America during the 1960s, in a period characterised by dictatorships and regimes which required complete obedience from the people to the State. The primary concern of liberation theology was the poor and the oppressed. In sharp contrast to the dominant theologies of the west, liberation theology took Jesus's message of liberation in the gospels as real. The notion of Jesus as liberator was an important message to those who lived in poverty and oppression. Liberation theology, therefore, exposes how traditional theology was produced in privileged or wealthy contexts, yet hunger and persecution characterised the social and economic locations of the majority of the world.

In 1971 Gustavo Gutiérrez, a Peruvian theologian, released *A Theology of Liberation*. He popularised the phrase that became a central motif of liberation theology, that God had a 'preferential option for the poor'. In the fight for economic justice, human rights, and an end to poverty, liberation theology looks at biblical narratives which show how God sided with the oppressed and marginalised. Ivan Petrella comments how Gutiérrez's theology was practical: 'Theology is a second step, commitment and participation in the struggles of marginalised communities is the first step' (Petrella, 2007: 162).

The liberation theology movement was criticised by the Roman Catholic Church. In 1979 Pope John Paul II stated how it was too close to secular Marxism. Marxism, from the economic and philosophical writings of Karl Marx (1818–1883), revealed how social class and conflict were a result of wealth and the powerful systems which produced wealth. The idea of liberation for the oppressed and marginalised became a lens used in feminist and gay and lesbian theologies. These are known as contextual theologies – theologies that are grounded in particular social contexts and experiences.

FEMINIST THEOLOGY

In the late 19th and early 20th centuries the first wave of feminism advanced issues of women's equality in the western world. Its focus was on allowing women the right to vote (suffrage) and on legal inequalities which favoured and were biased towards men. An example of this included the fight for a woman's right to own property, which was granted in the UK in 1882. Yet it was in the 1960s that a second wave of feminism drew attention to further important and timely issues including sexuality, workplace rights, reproductive rights, and the role of women in the family. It was during this period of second-wave feminism, which lasted approximately 20 years, that feminist concerns in relation to Christianity were voiced. Thus, the idea of feminist theology developed.

Feminist theology exposes and challenges the role of women within the Christian churches. Traditionally, the fact Jesus and his disciples were male was used to justify the subordination of women within the churches; for example, why women could not become priests. Throughout, feminist theology has also re-examined the role of women in the Bible, through feminist biblical interpretations. Scholars have examined women in the gospel stories at the time of Jesus, as well as their roles in the development of the early church. Feminist theology exposes how theology is soaked in assumptions and practices based on male experiences, and how theology is overwhelmingly authored by men. Patriarchy is a system by which men are privileged power holders and women are subjugated. The agenda of feminist theology is to dismantle patriarchal theology. Feminist theology, therefore, developed methodologies which prioritised and promoted women's experiences as a source of theology. Such experiences included discussions of motherhood, childbearing, sexual violence, and lesbianism. The turn to women's experiences highlights how traditional theology had been a source of oppression towards women.

One of the most prominent voices in feminist theology at the time of its emergence was Mary Daly. In 1968 Daly published *The Church and the Second Sex*, a critique of the Catholic Church. Daly's critique is formed from her observation of how the Church puts women on a pedestal, yet this pedestal renders women invisible at

the same time. Daly titles one chapter 'Pedestal Peddlers', exploring how women are encouraged to be selfless, hidden, and find
fulfilment in motherhood and as wives. Daly exposes how a
woman's role in Christianity is to be passive and silent, like the
Mary revered by the Church.

More radical explorations in feminist theology came from Daly
five years later. In 1973 she authored *Beyond God the Father*, a
critique of the Christian tradition as a model of patriarchy. Daly's
work reveals how the language used to talk about God is masculine (God the Father; God the Son) and this language is
therefore an obstacle for women. The patriarchy in Christianity
was exposed by Daly, who states 'if God is male then male is
God' (Daly, 1973: 19). In a shocking move, Daly claims that the
task of feminist theology was to castrate the male God of Christianity. She reveals how this male God is a source of oppression
and implicit in patriarchy. Daly's work also called for feminists to
reclaim Eve. Within the story of Genesis at the opening of the
Bible, Eve is associated with temptation, sin, and death. Daly calls
for feminist theologians to exorcise the association of woman
(Eve) with evil. She writes: 'Women as a caste are "Eve" and are
punished by a cohesive set of laws, customs and social arrange-
ments that enforce an all pervasive double standard' (1973: 62).

Daly exposes the problematic nature of the manhood of Jesus,
referring to Jesus as the God-man. This points to the problem that
the 'image of God' is male, as Daly says, and this image is reflected
in men's roles in politics and society. In such terms, the idea of
Jesus's maleness is in collusion with sexual hierarchy and patriarchy.
If idolatry is defined as the worship of false gods or idols, then
Daly's 'Christolatry' reveals that worshipping Jesus equates to
worshipping the male. According to Daly, women cannot accept
the idea of incarnation in the form of a male saviour.

It was not only Daly who had such concerns about Jesus as
male. Rosemary Radford Ruether engages with some of Daly's
concerns in her publication of *Sexism and God-Talk* in 1983.
Ruether famously asks, 'Can a male saviour save women?'
(Ruether, 1983: 116). She exposes how women's experiences
have been virtually excluded from theology and that theology
is based on male experience rather than human experience.
Ruether states:

> The uniqueness of feminist theology lies not in its use of the criterion of experience but rather in its use of women's experience, which has been almost entirely shut out of theological reflection in the past. The use of women's experience in feminist theology, therefore, explodes as a critical force, exposing classical theology, including its codified traditions, as based on male experience rather than on universal human experience (Ruether, 1983: 13).

In responding to her own question – 'can a male saviour save women?' – Ruether's answer is similar to the ideas found in liberation theology, as she envisages Christ as the liberator. In this role as liberator, Christ liberates women from oppression, just as he liberates the poor. The idea of Christian justice can therefore be applied to women. Ruether's work sets out an important agenda for feminist theology, as she states 'the critical principle of feminist theology is the promotion of the full humanity of women' (1983: 18). Her aim was to recover the neglected aspect of Christianity – the contributions and beliefs of women. Theology can then be constructed with feminist principles and women's experiences.

The idea of language used to talk about God as being masculine was still problematic for some in feminist theology. Sally McFague addresses the concern about male-centric language used to describe God and argues that language is a metaphor, stating how 'theology is mostly fiction' (McFague, 1987: xi). She envisages God as mother, lover, and friend, and uses female pronouns (she/her) to refer to God. Feminist theology, therefore, challenges traditional concepts of God.

The tensions between feminism and the patriarchal tradition of Christianity were beyond repair for some. In 1990 Daphne Hampson authored *Theology and Feminism*. In it she reaches the conclusion that Christian theology and feminism are incompatible. For Hampson, the sexism within Christianity means it is beyond repair, despite the work of feminist theologians. She states: 'an observant friend of mine once remarked that whereas Christian feminists want to change the actors in the play, what I want is a different kind of play' (Hampson, 1990: 162). Because of this incompatibility, she describes her theology as 'post-Christian'. Identifying as post-Christian means that the theologian chooses to distance herself from the language and assumptions of Christianity.

LESBIAN AND GAY LIVES

In the late 1940s and early 1950s scientific studies in human sexuality revealed pioneering insights into sexual behaviours. Sexologist Alfred Kinsey conducted two major research projects in human sexuality (Kinsey et al., 1948; Kinsey et al., 1953). It is important to note that at the time of his publications it was illegal to be gay in the UK and USA. Kinsey's results led to new thinking, firstly that biological genitalia do not equate to sexuality, and, secondly, that sexuality is not limited to a binary (hetero/homo) but that there is, rather, a sexual continuum.

Despite this work, in the history of homosexuality we see how to be gay or lesbian was once considered a psychological disorder and was treated like an illness. To be gay was to be sick. Medical interventions attempted to establish cures for such an illness, with the aim of transforming sick gay or lesbian people into healthy heterosexuals. Procedures to 'cure' at this time were very invasive, with lasting physical and psychological damage. In some examples, gay men underwent castration and lesbians suffered genital mutilation, while shock treatment and hypnosis were also used as experiments with the aim of offering a 'cure' to non-heterosexual people. This also extends to the practice of gay conversion therapy, an attempt to make a gay-identifying individual convert to be heterosexual using spiritual interventions.

Against the social backdrop of feminist activism, lesbian and gay political movements began to stand up against the anti-gay legal system. One major example of such activism took place in a New York bar, the Stonewall Inn, and became known as the Stonewall riots. The bar was known as a safe and affirming place for gay and lesbian customers, but it was subjected to routine police raids. On 28 June 1969, during one such raid, the patrons fought back against police harassment and this led to four days of intense rioting. News of the riots at Stonewall spread, and for many it was a call to activism. Historians and anthropologists are aware of inconsistencies in attempting to document the events at Stonewall: a generation of those at Stonewall died during the AIDS crisis of the 1980s; the riots were disorganised; people were intoxicated; and lots of people claimed to be there as they were aware of its importance as a major event in LGBTQ+ history (see Carter, 2004). Despite debates about actual facts, Stonewall was undoubtedly a major turning point for LGBTQ+ empowerment. Gay rights groups grew across the country, including the Gay Liberation Front (GLF) comprised of activists for sexual liberation. The GLF spread to the UK and Canada, and the first Gay Pride event took place in New York in 1970 to mark the one-year anniversary of the riots. By 1971, Pride events took place in numerous states across the USA and within European cities such as London, Paris, and West Berlin. Whereas gay and lesbian liberation movements moved towards events known as Pride, there was still, for many, a personal and social shame attached to same-sex orientations. Arguably the whole point of the Pride events was to counter interior feelings of shame. 'Pride' as an emotion becomes a counter-balance to 'shame'. The idea of shame has its own emotional and psychological consequences, as LGBTQ+ people can often lead hidden lives or not be open about their relationships with family, friends or colleagues. This shame can also be a religious or spiritual shame or inner conflict.

GAY AND LESBIAN THEOLOGIES

Alongside gay and lesbian liberation movements, in theology lesbian and gay voices began to speak. Susannah Cornwall is right to note how those who produced lesbian and gay theologies were activist prophets:

> Lesbian and gay theologies, and those who have produced and inhabited them over the years, continue to stand prophetically themselves as testimony to God's good work in non-heterosexual lives and relationships (Cornwall, 2011: 68).

To a large extent the lineage of queer theologies can be traced back to pathways paved by liberation, feminist, and lesbian and gay theologies. One of the very earliest examples of gay and lesbian theology was a collection of essays entitled *Is Gay Good? Ethics, Theology and Homosexuality*, published in 1971. The essays considered questions of ethics, pastoral responses, Christian positions, the role of the Church, and the theological idea of love. In the volume, Del Martin and Phyllis Lyon wrote a significant essay entitled 'A Lesbian Approach to Theology'. They were a lesbian couple living in the USA who were committed to the feminist and gay rights movements. Their paper offered a reminder that the 'homosexual too is a child of God' (Martin & Lyon, 1971: 219).

Within the decades that followed in the USA, gay male theologians also began to put pen to paper in the spirit of activism. Gary David Comstock wrote *Gay Theology Without Apology* (Comstock, 1993). He used personal narrative to articulate the negative impact of theology and church teaching on gay men. Comstock states that biblical interpretations are saturated in heterosexism and patriarchy which are damaging to gay men and lesbians:

> Within such a patriarchal framework, therefore, lesbians and gay men should not be surprised to find passages that malign us. Our tendency, however, has been to apologize for those biblical passages that appear to condemn homosexuality and attack lesbians and gay men (Comstock, 1993: 38).

The theme of intimate relationships as a source for the community runs through Comstock's text, observing that relationships are orchestrated by God. He states, 'I believe that we are created and destroyed in our relationships. God is the mutuality and reciprocity in our relationships, the compelling and transforming power that brings together, reconciles, and creates us' (1993: 127).

In the UK, Sean Gill edited a collection of essays, *The Lesbian and Gay Christian Movement* (Gill, 1998). In one essay, USA-based scholar Robert Goss discusses the post-Christian turn for feminist scholars and gay and lesbian Christians who have moved into a form of exile by leaving mainstream denominational groups. Goss states how this is like 'rearranging deck chairs on the *Titanic*' (Goss, 1998: 192). He asks, 'Can we create a Christianity that escapes from its heritage of violence and from its irrelevancy in addressing the spiritual needs of gays/lesbians?' (1998: 192). This question underpins part of the agenda of lesbian and gay theologies.

In the quest for sexual justice, lesbian and gay activists worked together in union. Although this alliance was helpful in many ways, some remained concerned by the collapse of lesbian and gay experiences. By putting them together, as 'lesbian and gay', identities were diluted or lost. Elizabeth Stuart highlights the tensions between gay and lesbian theologies:

> Gay theology began to emerge in the 1970s as gay Christians started
> to reflect theologically upon the gay liberation movement. In its early
> days such reflection was dominated by men who felt able to do
> theology about and on behalf of lesbians (Stuart, 2003: 15).

Indeed, the tensions went beyond a claim to voice. While collectively lesbians and gays shared a common struggle against homophobia and heterosexism, some feminists were aware how gay men remained connected to issues of patriarchy and still enjoyed male privilege. Stuart observes how gay men were 'regarded as implicated in the structures of patriarchy' (Stuart, 2003: 7). Elsewhere she explains some of the general tensions between gay and lesbian theologies:

> Very broadly speaking, gay men often seemed content to seek a place
> at the Christian table, using already existent and accepted theological
> concepts and arguments to gain that place. Lesbian theologies, how-
> ever, wanted to overturn the whole table. They argued that Christian
> theology was too rooted in patriarchy, racism, heterosexism and other
> exclusionary beliefs and practices, and that it would have to be rebuilt
> if it were to be truly liberating (Stuart, 1997: 2–3).

In the gay and lesbian theologies produced around the time of the millennium it is clear that the influence of queer theory and queer theologies begin to take hold. Robert Goss's *Jesus Acted Up: A Gay and Lesbian Manifesto* (1993), for example, uses the term queer in a political sense, reflecting its use in the activist movement. For Goss, queer was used as an expression of radical activism. Within his manifesto Goss tackles the themes of homophobia, HIV/AIDS, and sexual justice. In a similar vein to ideas in liberation and feminist theology, Goss sees Christ, formed by patriarchal traditional theology, as an oppressor, but the person of Jesus as a liberator. With a commitment to practical theology, Goss's work examines how Christians can live their faith in queer Christian communities. In the final chapter he states how 'queer anger is holy anger. It's time to be angry […] Queer Christians need to follow in the steps of Jesus […] They need to act up against the churches and stop the hatred' (Goss, 1993: 177).

One of the defining transition periods between gay and lesbian theologies and queer theologies is found in Elizabeth Stuart's *Gay and Lesbian Theologies: Repetitions with Christian Difference* (Stuart, 2003). It serves as an excellent bridging text revealing how gay and lesbian theologies differ from queer theologies. Stuart explains how gay and lesbian theologies had reached a point of stalemate and that something more radical was required: 'gay and lesbian theology reaches a state of theological breakdown and this is manifested in its tendency to repeat itself' (2003: 11). She uses the French term *répétition*, which, as well as meaning 'repetition' in English, also means 'rehearsal'. Stuart states how gay and lesbian theologies have served as a rehearsal, 'a preparation for something more theologically radical' (2003: 11). This radical theology is revealed as queer theology, or queer theologies.

THE RISE OF QUEER THEORY

The rise of queer theory must not be viewed solely as a development rooted in the transformative brilliance of the 20th century's critical thinkers. Queer theory developed alongside hard-fought activism from second-wave feminism and the gay and lesbian liberation movements discussed above. The theory which began to germinate in academic settings was nourished by the social and political climate of the day.

Queer theory disrupts long-held notions of binary gender and sexual identities. As a theory it is known for its complex language and ideas. In order to provide a 'way in' to this philosophical area, below I trace the very basics in the development of philosophical thought which preceded and influenced the emergence of 'queer theory' as well as describing the agenda of queer.

In the middle of the 20th century in Europe, *structuralism* was a popular method that explored how human life and culture was understood in relation to wider structures. So, instead of looking at 'things' as separate items, structuralism focused on the relationship between things. In one example, the word 'light' exists because of its relationship to 'dark'. So, the word 'light' itself does not just describe what it is, but it also describes what it is not. This relationship helps to place it in the structure of things. In one sense, structuralism claims that naming an object describes both presence and absence. Structuralism, therefore, works to examine the limitations of meaning. Ferdinand de Saussure explained this distinction as 'signifier' and 'signified'. The signifier is the word used – for example, 'light' – while the signified is a mental concept that extends beyond the word itself. 'Dark' is one of these many concepts which may emerge in this case. Another example of the relationship between signifier and signified is how red roses come to signify love. This focus on systems or structures led to an understanding of objects within binary structures; the most obvious example of this was 'male/female'. Structuralism was a method based on systems, stability, order, rules, and discipline.

Following engagement with de Saussure and structuralist thinking, *post-structuralism* countered these claims of stable, universal truths and claimed there were more possibilities than simply those that exist in binary structures. The Algerian-born philosopher Jacques Derrida became one of the major figures associated with post-structuralism in 1960s' France. Derrida is often referred to as 'the father of deconstruction', as his methods of deconstruction began to have a significant impact on studies across academic disciplines. Derrida would claim that the method of deconstruction is impossible to define. In post-structuralism, Derrida showed how definitions are dangerous as they do not point to what something means, but how they come to mean it. Deconstruction, therefore, went against normal and accepted readings of texts. Texts in this sense do not just mean literary documents, but include different con*texts* – texts can be events, situations, media, people. Context refers to who we are, where we are, and when we are. With different contexts come different possibilities, so there is never a real structure or a real truth, but there are multiple possibilities of interpreting the text or context. Deconstruction is the method of engaging with how a text gets its meaning and how such meanings are unstable. Derrida is famous for saying 'there is no out-of-context' (*il n'y a pas de hors-texte*). In very simplified terms, Derrida claims that texts mean just what we want them to mean and we arrive at such meaning from our own positions – who we are, where we are, when we are. There is no final say on a text; there is no final destination.

Post-structuralists deconstruct texts. The method of deconstruction challenged western culture and was a major concept within emerging philosophical movements. By focusing on context, deconstruction questioned 'normal', assumed meanings; it removed binary thinking and hierarchies by showing how 'structures' were not really stable. There is no single truth about who we are, but there are multiple interpretations. Post-structuralist thought is therefore highly critical of claims to truth, including claims from science and religion.

Essentialism is a term used to describe a set of characteristics which serve to denote an identity 'group'. Within the 20th century, significant French philosophers (Sartre, de Beauvoir, Camus, Merleau-Ponty) questioned the idea that people's identities are designated at birth (biological essentialism). They also questioned that identities were created through childhood experiences (social essentialism). Deconstruction challenges categories of essentialism in identity, such as race, gender, sexuality, class. It demonstrates how each category of identity is not universal, or 'true'. Post-structuralist thinking sees identity as culturally and socially formed. Rather than identity being essentialised, we occupy categories of identity.

Alongside Derrida, Michel Foucault is another thinker credited for his contribution to contemporary thought and philosophy. Foucault was a critical thinker who published on mental illness, history, sexuality, power, and the prison system. He revealed how power and knowledge are inextricably connected in his text *Discipline and Punish* (Foucault, 1977), which is considered by many to be a landmark in postmodernist thought. According to Foucault, power produces knowledge, and he uses the example of a prison to demonstrate how power structures in society reflect those of a prison. This example extends to power structures in other public institutions such as schools, hospitals, factories. One of his main examples was to use the idea of a panopticon – a tower within a prison which acts as a constant form of surveillance of prisoners. Because of this continuous monitoring, prisoners would regulate their own conduct, knowing they were being seen. Rather than focusing on this as a tool for the corrective services of prisons, the panopticon can be used to illustrate how people modify their own behaviours in society based on the perceived critical gazes from others. Because of an individual's awareness of these constant critical gazes, people self-regulate in their presentation and behaviours as a means to avoid negative responses, humiliation, and disapproval. In brief, the panopticon is the regulator of what is considered to be 'normal'. Foucault calls this process 'power-knowledge', as the power does not come from a top-down hierarchy but, rather, that ideas are shared subtly and people self-regulate because of them.

In his pivotal work, *The History of Sexuality: Volume 1*, Foucault explores this idea in relation to sex, seeing the connection between sex and knowledge. He extends this idea to the accepted understanding of 'sexuality', as sexuality was produced by power-knowledge relations such as science and religion. Foucault himself had experienced same-sex relations and was fully aware of the social and legal positions which constrained gay relationships and expressions of sexuality. He notes how social systems construct sexual identity by making it central to an individual's character. Foucault takes the idea of homosexuality being seen as an identity, and not as an act to do with bodies or pleasure. For heterosexuality to be normalised and dominant it needs an 'other' to which it can exist, and upon which it relies for its normalised status (Foucault, 1976: 110). Therefore, Foucault was able to demonstrate how the homosexual person was constructed, rendering homosexuality profoundly threatening by establishing it as (the inherently 'abnormal') 'other'. Because it is considered as an identity, it then is subjected to interpretations from institutions, such as medicine, law, and even religion. Thus, ideas of heterosexuality as 'natural' and non-heterosexual sexualities as 'unnatural' come about. Sexuality is therefore regulated by power dynamics, rather than being part of a person's essence.

In postmodernist thought, the lens of power-knowledge is focused firmly on the human body, so aspects of identity – such as gender, sexuality, race, age, dis/ability, appearance – are all regulated by self and others, thereby producing the idea of 'normal'. Postmodernism, therefore, calls attention to the idea of there being no 'truth', as knowledge is produced in contextual systems of multiple power structures. Where there is power, there is resistance. This idea of power-knowledge is mirrored in the task of queering theology and examining the relationship between queer theologies and dominant mainstream theologies.

FEMINIST, WOMANIST, AND 'QUEER' THEORISTS

In addition to critical theories emerging about post-structuralism and postmodernism in France, a number of second-wave feminist and womanist thinkers are credited for their contribution to emerging queer thought, even though it was not considered or labelled 'queer' at the time. These feminist and womanist thinkers include Adrienne Rich, Monique Wittig, Gayle Rubin, Audre Lorde, bell hooks, and Judith Butler.

In 1980 Adrienne Rich examined heterosexuality through a critical lens. She wrote 'Compulsory Heterosexuality and Lesbian Identity', arguing how heterosexuality functions as a social power and that people are pressured into seeing heterosexuality as the norm. Rich notes how 'the ideology of heterosexual romance, beamed at her from childhood out of fairy tales, television, films, advertising, popular songs, wedding pageantry' (Rich, 1980: 645) is part of social conditioning. People conform to heterosexuality, according to Rich, because they gain benefits from doing so, and there are losses to those who deviate from it. Rich coined the term 'compulsory heterosexuality' to describe how people conform, a term popularised throughout further queer texts. In her essay, Rich was highly critical of patriarchal gender relations, where men dominate. Her work introduced the idea of a 'lesbian continuum' as a way to see the bonds and relationships between women, not only as same-sex attraction. Despite its significant critical reading of heterosexuality, Rich's work was criticised for focusing solely on lesbian experience rather than wider marginalised sexualities.

As Rich focused on matters of sexuality, Gayle Rubin's influential paper 'Thinking Sex' (Rubin, 1984) explored the multidimensional nature of human sexuality in the form of a sex hierarchy. This hierarchy is regulated by different aspects of society: religion, law, the media, mainstream culture. In thinking about sex, Rubin establishes a 'charmed circle' of sex which is validated by words such as 'normal', 'natural', 'healthy'. This charmed circle of sexuality includes sex which is heterosexual, marital, monogamous, reproductive. In contrast, Rubin describes the negativity associated with certain types of sexual behaviours, such as lesbian and gay relationships, sex workers, and pornography. These 'outer limits' work in opposition to the charmed circle, and sex in these categories is deemed 'abnormal', 'unnatural', 'unhealthy'. Rubin defines the sex hierarchy as an erotic pyramid:

> Marital, reproductive heterosexuals are alone at the top of the erotic pyramid. Clamoring below are unmarried monogamous heterosexuals in couples, followed by most other heterosexuals. Solitary sex floats ambiguously [...] Stable, long-term lesbian and gay male couples are verging on respectability, but bar dykes and promiscuous gay men are hovering just above the groups at the very bottom of the pyramid. The most despised sexual castes currently include transsexuals, transvestites, fetishists, sadomasochists, sex workers such as prostitutes and porn models, and the lowliest of all, those whose eroticism transgresses generational boundaries (Rubin, 1984: 279).

For Rubin, writing in the 1980s, the work of gay and lesbian movements was invested in assimilationist politics, as they worked for social integration. That means that such groups wanted to be similar to and have the same rights as heterosexuals. Rubin sees such assimilation as problematic, as the scramble to enter the 'charmed circle' still means that other groups are marginalised and remain at the outer limits. Such groups are then further oppressed because of this 'abnormal' status. Rubin cites organised religion, naming Christianity, as contributing to teaching that sex is sinful.

In 1991, 11 years after Rich's treatise on compulsory heterosexuality, Monique Wittig authored *The Straight Mind*, which exposes how heterosexuality forms part of the everyday practices of life: thinking, speaking, feeling. Because assumed heterosexuality is widespread, it is pervasive. This points to why non-heterosexuality has been deemed so deviant and alien. Indeed, Wittig argues that because heterosexuality is so dominant in culture, its power is invisible. Non-heterosexuals therefore examine themselves in relation to this. Wittig's work was popularised by her controversial statement that 'lesbians are not women' (Wittig, 1991: 32). She is critical that the idea of 'woman' referred to the sexual, procreative function of women. In using this idea of reproduction, Wittig states how matriarchy is just as heterosexual as patriarchy. For Wittig, being a 'woman' only makes sense in a straight world, when people think of heterosexual women, 'as "woman" has meaning only in heterosexual systems of thought' (1991: 32).

Complementing these positions were the voices of Black feminist thinkers, who raised awareness that the civil rights movement, which campaigned to end discrimination and segregation on the basis of race, had overlooked the question of gender. Comparatively, the feminist movement had also neglected issues of race. In this way their work questioned the idea of 'identity' as a universal term, as there were wide-ranging experiences between 'women' based on class and race.

Audre Lorde was a Black lesbian feminist socialist who revealed the notion of privilege between women based on class, race, and age in her essay 'Age, Race, Class and Sex: Women Redefining Difference' (Lorde, 1984). Lorde points to the actions of oppression, noting how 'it is the responsibility of the oppressed to teach the oppressors their mistakes' (1984: 114). In highlighting privilege, Lorde exposes the irony of the marginalised teaching the dominant: how Black people are expected to educate white people about race; how women educate men about gender; how gay and lesbian people educate straight people about sexuality. For Lorde, the category of 'women' had been based on the experiences of white women, to which Black women are 'other'. Lorde states:

> As a Black lesbian feminist comfortable with the many different ingredients of my identity, and a woman committed to racial and sexual freedom from oppression, I find I am constantly being encouraged to pluck out some one aspect of myself and present this as the meaningful whole, eclipsing or denying the other parts of self. But this is a destructive and fragmenting way to live (Lorde, 1984: 210).

The term 'womanist' was coined by Alice Walker to describe Black feminists, and is grounded in the history, culture, and experiences of Black women. The term removes the white assumptions of feminism. bell hooks, the American author, feminist, and socialist published *Ain't I a Woman? Black Women and Feminism* (bell hooks, 1981) and *Feminist Theory: From Margin to Center* (bell hooks, 1984). hooks' work on gender and feminism reveals how, in the quest for women to be assimilated to men, the task is futile, as women are not all equal to one another. hooks challenged feminism to look at how issues of gender interacted with race, class, and sex. Her work also insisted that men must be part of the campaign for equality. Lorde's and hooks' work therefore formed the basis for ideas of how certain forms of oppression intersect with other forms of oppression; a term we understand now as intersectionality, due to the work of Kimberlé Crenshaw. So, an individual may be marginalised because of one identity characteristic, but that is further compacted when others are examined. Intersectionality shows how systems of oppression and discrimination are multiple. The most marginalised people, therefore, fall under multiple minority groups. Writings from feminist and womanist thinkers were critical in the development of thinking (contesting categories of identity and exploring issues of marginalisation) which later came to characterise queer theory.

Judith Butler is often credited as one of the founders of queer thought, but Butler did not see herself in this position. Her work on the identity of 'woman' demonstrates her troubling of gender categories. In 1990 Butler's *Gender Trouble* built on the intellectual theories from French critical thinkers, including Foucault. Butler's thought dismantles essentialist ideas of gender, stating that gender is not fixed biologically, and that people are not born male or female, but born into a body. Butler states how gender is socially constructed: society and culture had built ideas of what it is to be male or female, and individuals perform these ideas. On a simple level, what we think of masculine or feminine are performed by individuals, especially in terms of appearance and in the clothes that people wear. In revealing that gender is not a biological fact, Butler develops the notion of 'gender performativity'. Miriam Meyerhoff offers a helpful definition of how performativity is different from performance:

> The performative quality of gender and sexuality is distinct from gendered and sexualized performance. If a performance is something controlled and possibly characterized by a degree of artifice, performativity is talking about something completely different. To say that gender is performative is simply to say that how we understand gender, and how we position ourselves as gendered or sexual beings in relation to others is achieved through the repetition and enactment of these activities (Meyerhoff, 2014: 2).

Gender is, therefore, less to do with genitalia or sex assigned at birth, but it is an act which people perform and repeat. Perceptions of gender are repetitions which are being repeated individually and collectively. For Butler, gender is what you do, rather than who you are.

The coining of the term 'queer theory' is often attributed to Teresa de Lauretis, who used the words 'queer theory' in a special edition of the feminist cultural journal *Differences* (de Lauretis, 1991). Her title, 'Queer Theory: Lesbian and Gay Sexualities', shows how de Lauretis's focus at the time was on issues of sexuality, whereas queer theory today moves beyond that and ruptures all ideas of identity. Nonetheless, the word 'queer' quickly became applied to critical thought around issues of gender and sexuality in the 1990s. Building on the thoughts of Rich's 'compulsory heterosexuality' and Rubin's work on gender and sex, Michel Warner edited *Fear of a Queer Planet* (Warner, 1993) and used the word 'heteronormative' to refer to the idea that heterosexuality had been so normalised by society. Heteronormativity describes the assumption that people are heterosexual and how society presumes heterosexuality. One way to describe the reach of heteronormativity is how non-heterosexuals or non-cisgender people 'come out'. The act of coming out is unique to non-normative people, even today, which renders heterosexuality the norm. It is important to note that 'compulsory heterosexuality' and 'heteronormativity' differ. Heteronormativity is the assumption that everyone is straight, whereas compulsory heterosexuality describes the process and enforcement of heteronormativity through the constant messages that promote and uphold it.

Another emerging critical thinker at this time was Eve Kosofsky Sedgwick. Her essay, 'How To Bring Your Kids Up Gay' (Sedgwick, 1991), critiques how homosexuality has been pathologised and thought of as abnormal. Sedgwick calls attention to the false presumption that binary gender equates to binary sexuality. In considering how being homosexual may be seen as acceptable among adults in society, Sedgwick notes that there is an institutional agenda among psychoanalysts that children who may grow up to be gay should still be treated and dissuaded. In *Epistemology of the Closet* (Sedgwick, 1990), she states how binary definitions of gender and sexuality are far too limiting and simplistic to be able to represent human sexuality. 'The closet' is a metaphor for hidden homosexuality, where those who experience same-sex attraction attempt to hide and conceal their sexuality. Using examples taken from literature, Sedgwick argues that despite the stigma and the consequences individuals face from society, people are at their most liberated when they leave the closet and close its door.

There are power relations at play in the performativity of gender and regulation of sexuality. What come to be considered 'normal' or 'natural' only do so because they have been performed by a majority and repeated. The work of the theorists highlighted above collectively reveals how gender and sexuality are no longer seen as essential or fixed, but socially constructed and fluid. In a similar way, Christianity and Christian theology have been constructed by power relations and are seen as fixed in some way only because of dominant repetitions. Queer theologies rupture these repetitions.

Although, in its development, queer theory first concerned itself with marginalised gender and sexualities, queer theory now moves beyond this. Queer is a much-contested term and cannot be easily defined. Where definitions exist, they fail to recognise that queer is fluid; it is unfixable. David Halperin illustrates how the term queer cannot be easily defined:

> Queer is by definition whatever is at odds with the normal, the legitimate, the dominant. There is nothing in particular to which it necessarily refers. It is an identity without an essence (Halperin, 1995: 62).

Halperin goes on to say that queer is a positionality rather than an identity. Such a positionality means that it is not limited to LGBTQ+ people but can be taken up by anyone. Anything which challenges compulsory ideas of binary gender and heterosexuality can be queer. In his edited book, *Straight with a Twist* (Thomas, 2000), Calvin Thomas explores how queer theory interrogates heterosexuality and how it includes and speaks for straight people too. This is further developed in Chapter 5.

As queer is indefinable, instead of looking at what queer *is* it is better to look at what queer *does*. Or, even better, what queer 'undoes'. These are the most common ways queer theory has come to be applied:

[i]   queer resists ideas of categorisation;
[ii] queer challenges the idea of essentialism;
[iii] queer challenges 'normal';
[iv] queer removes binary thinking and presumptions;
[v]   queer exposes and disrupts power relations or hierarchies.

[I] QUEER RESISTS IDEAS OF CATEGORISATION

We have seen how queer goes beyond being a descriptor for non-heterosexual identities. Queer resists all definitions and categories. Annamarie Jagose states how 'queer itself can have neither a fundamental logic, nor a consistent set of characteristics' (Jagose, 1996: 96), so queer itself cannot be defined. To be defined means to be normalised! Queer resists definitions because any attempt to define it limits it. Therefore, queer resists categorisation.

[II] QUEER CHALLENGES THE IDEA OF ESSENTIALISM

Essentialism refers to the idea that there are a set of fixed, uniform characteristics to identity. Identity therefore becomes universal. In her work on feminist identity, Elizabeth Spelman states how 'one's gender identity is not related to one's racial and class identity as the parts of pop-bead necklaces are related, separable and insertable in other "strands" with different racial and class parts' (Spelman, 1988: 15). Queer challenges the ideas of essentialism, therefore, as each aspect of an individual's identity cannot be 'popped off' and examined, without seeing how one part relates to another. The idea of an identity having a fixed essence is therefore false.

[III] QUEER CHALLENGES 'NORMAL'

The work of Foucault and Butler showed how identities are enmeshed within systems of social power and control, which regulate what is understood as 'normal'. Heteronormativity is socially powerful. It reveals how heterosexuality is presumed within society as the dominant expression of sexuality and this is tied up in institutional life: law, business, education, health. The same is true for gender, as cisgender has been considered the norm. Queer reveals how biological sex does not equate to gender. What is accepted as a norm has been socially constructed. What we think of as fixed categories are not fixed at all. They are only fixed by imagination and social conditioning. Queer challenges any assumption of normal by enlarging the picture and looking at the experiences of those on the margins to see how the idea of 'normal' is ruptured.

[IV] QUEER DISRUPTS BINARY THINKING AND PRESUMPTION

Identity categories such as man/woman and heterosexual/homo-sexual actually serve to reinforce heteronormativity, as they only allow for thinking in opposites. Such categories operate around a norm; so homosexuality, for example, operates around the norm of heterosexuality. Queer removes binary thinking and assumptions. Binaries are limiting. Queer pushes beyond binaries by showing that gender, for example, is not just male/female. There are people who identify as trans, agender, gender-fluid, for example.

[V] QUEER EXPOSES AND DISRUPTS POWER RELATIONS OR HIERARCHIES

Queer exposes the power relations that are often invisible in society and religion. Queer examines how power has been used in reg-ulating what is considered 'normal'. Queer works against patriarchy and heteronormativity by exposing how these systems privilege certain individuals over others. Traditionally, privilege has served white, heterosexual, cisgender males. Queer exposes such privilege and this disruption can serve as a catalyst and agent of change.

THE APPLICATION OF QUEER THEORY

Queer has come to mean different things: queer as a catch-all term for LGBTQ+ identities and queer as a theory. There has been concern about queer theory being a highly philosophical task, rather than working at a grassroots level to serve individuals who experience marginalisation. The language used in queer theory writings is often dense, complex, and unfamiliar to anyone starting out in the area. Biblical scholar Deryn Guest expresses concern in relation to the language used 'that this can render queer biblical and theological scholarship a heavily theorized, jargon-ridden, highfalutin language game that loses the wider audience' (Guest, 2018: 440).

Not only does this create a divide between those who have been afforded the opportunity of education to be able to tackle such chal-lenging work, it begs the question as to who this intellectualism is for? If it is not accessible to non-academic people, does it not lose its political power and agency? Elsewhere, Guest notes how complex language can create divisions:

> Queer will prove to be an elitist discourse, hardly accessible to the lay person or in touch with the lived realities of grassroots communities [...] Despite the argument that complex ideas require complex terminology, some feminists have long upheld a commitment to the communities they seek to represent and to present their ideas in ways that are accessible to such communities (Guest, 2005: 51).

Guest suggests that the language of queer should be accessible. Queer theologian Marcella Althaus-Reid shared the same concerns, questioning 'queer theologies as a luxury which only privileged women in academia can afford to pursue' (Althaus-Reid, 2008: 106). Questions of education, class, and intellectualism can, therefore, create power structures of their own, as well as systems of exclusion and marginalisation.

CONCLUSION

This chapter has navigated key concepts in the development of queer studies in the 20th century. The activism, resistance, and protest from feminist and lesbian and gay groups paved the way for social justice for marginalised groups. Against this backdrop, feminist theory, womanist theory, feminist theology, and gay and lesbian theologies interrogated traditional Christian understandings of gender and sexuality, exposing its patriarchal and heteronormative power structures. Queer theory exposes heteronormative assumptions within society and culture. Queer theologies undo traditional theology by deconstructing it, by critiquing the patriarchy and heteronormative assumptions at play in its production. Queer theologies liberate Christianity from the bondage of patriarchy and heteronormativity. Having undertaken a brief history of the development of queer theologies, Chapter 2 explores the queering of 'traditional' theology.

FURTHER READING AND ONLINE RESOURCES

Barker, M. J. and Scheele, J. (2016) *Queer: A Graphic History*. London: Icon Books.

A very accessible introduction to the development of queer theory. The text is written without complex language and the discussion is illuminated by cartoon drawings illustrating key ideas.

Cornwall, S. (2011) *Controversies in Queer Theology*. London: SCM Press.

Cornwall examines key issues in queer theology in this detailed volume. This is a text highly recommended as the next step for those wishing to go beyond 'the basics'.

Goss, R. E. (1993) *Jesus Acted Up: A Gay and Lesbian Manifesto*. San Francisco: Harper.

Goss's manifesto calls for justice for, rather than acceptance of, lesbian and gay people by the churches. His book examines the importance for lesbian and gay Christians to reject institutional religion and embrace the Jesus found in the gospels. An iconic text in the history of Christian and sexual identities.

Stuart, E. (2003) *Gay and Lesbian Theologies: Repetitions and Critical Difference*. Hampshire: Ashgate.

This significant text offers a detailed and comprehensive overview of the histories of gay and lesbian theologies to queer theologies.

https://www.queertheology.com/

This website is aimed at Christians who are looking to reconcile their faith with their LGBTQ+ identities. It is aimed at supporting church groups in welcoming LGBTQ+ members. It does not engage with queer theology from a theoretical perspective.

REFERENCES

Althaus-Reid, M. (2008) 'The Bi/girl Writings: From Feminist Theology to Queer Theologies', in Isherwood, L. and McPhillips, K. (Eds.) *Post-Christian Feminisms: A Critical Approach*, pp. 105–116. Aldershot: Ashgate.
Butler, J. (1990) *Gender Trouble*. London: Routledge Classics [2006 print].
Carter, D. A. (2004) *Stonewall: The Riots That Sparked The Gay Revolution*. New York: St Martin's Griffin.
Comstock, G. D. (1993) *Gay Theology Without Apology*. Cleveland: Pilgrim Press.
Cornwall, S. (2011) *Controversies in Queer Theology*. London: SCM Press.
Crenshaw, K. (1989) Demarginalizing the Intersection of Race and Sex: A Black Feminist Critique of Antidiscrimination Doctrine, Feminist Theory

and Antiracist Politics. *University of Chicago Legal Forum*, 1(8). Available at: http://chicagounbound.uchicago.edu/uclf/vol1989/iss1/8

Daly, M. (1968) *The Church and the Second Sex*. Boston: Beacon Press.

Daly, M. (1973) *Beyond God the Father. Towards a Philosophy of Women's Liberation*. London: The Women's Press.

de Lauretis, T. (1991) Queer theory: Lesbian and gay sexualities. *Differences: Journal of Feminist Cultural Studies*, 3(2), pp. iii–xviii.

Foucault, M. (1976) *The History of Sexuality: 1: The Will to Knowledge*. London: Penguin.

Foucault, M. (1977) *Discipline and Punish: The Birth of the Prison* (trans. Alan Sheridan). Harmondsworth: Penguin.

Gill, S. (1998) *The Lesbian and Gay Christian Movement: Campaigning for Justice, Truth and Love*. London: Continuum.

Goss, R. E. (1993) *Jesus Acted Up. A Gay and Lesbian Manifesto*. San Francisco: Harper.

Goss, R. E. (1998) 'Sexual Visionaries and Freedom Fighters', in Gill, S. (Ed.) *The Lesbian and Gay Christian Movement: Campaigning for Justice, Truth and Love*, pp. 187–202. London: Continuum.

Guest, D. (2005) *When Deborah Met Jael: Lesbian Biblical Hermeneutics*. London: SCM Press.

Guest, D. (2018) Review of Sexual Disorientations: Queer Temporalities, Affects, Theologies, by Brintnall, K., Marchal, J. and Moore, S. (Eds.) in *Reviews in Religion and Theology*, 25(3), pp. 439–442.

Gutiérrez, G. (1971) *A Theology of Liberation*. Maryknoll: Orbis (translation in 1973, originally published as *Teología de la liberación: Perspectivas*. Lima: CEP, 1971).

Halperin, D. (1995) *Saint Foucault: Towards A Gay Hagiography*. Oxford: Oxford University Press.

Hampson, D. (1990) *Theology and Feminism*. London: Blackwell.

hooks, b. (1981) *Ain't I a Woman? Black Women and Feminism*. Boston: South End Press.

hooks, b. (1984). *Feminist Theory: From Margin to Center*. London: Pluto Press.

Jagose, A. (1996) *Queer Theory*. Melbourne: Melbourne University Press.

Kinsey, A., Pomeroy, W., Martin, C. and de Cly, E. M. (1948) *Sexual Behavior in the Human Female*, Philadelphia: W. B. Saunders.

Kinsey, A., Pomeroy, W., Martin, C. and Gebhard, P. (1953) *Sexual Behavior in the Human Female*. Philadelphia: W. B. Saunders.

Lorde, A. (1984) 'Age, Race, Class, and Sex: Women Redefining Difference', in Lorde, A. (Ed.) *Sister Outsider: Essays and Speeches*, pp. 114–123. California: Crossing Press.

Martin, D. and Lyon, P. (1971) 'A Lesbian Approach to Theology', in Oberholtzer, W. D. (Ed.) *Is Gay Good? Ethics, Theology and Homosexuality*, pp. 213–220. Philadelphia: Westminster Press.

McFague, S. (1987) *Models of God: Theology for An Ecological, Nuclear Age*. Philadelphia: Fortress Press.

Meyerhoff, M. (2014) 'Gender Performativity', in Whelehan, P. and Bolin, A. (Eds.) *The International Encyclopedia of Human Sexuality*, pp. 1–4. New Jersey: John Wiley & Sons. Available at: https://onlinelibrary.wiley.com/doi/full/10.1002/9781118896877.wbiehs178

Oberholtzer, W. D. (Ed.) (1971) *Is Gay Good? Ethics, Theology and Homosexuality*. Philadelphia: Westminster Press.

Petrella, I. (2007) 'Theology and Liberation: Juan Luis Segundo and Three Takes on Secular Inventiveness', in Althaus-Reid, M., Petrella, I. and Susin, L. C. (Eds.) *Another Possible World*, pp. 162–177. London: SCM Press.

Rich, A. (1980) Compulsory Heterosexuality and Lesbian Existence. *Signs*, 5(4), pp. 631–660.

Rubin, G. (1984) 'Thinking Sex: Notes for a Radical Theory of the Politics of Sexuality', in Vance, C. S. (Ed.) *Pleasure and Danger: Exploring Female Sexuality*, pp. 267–319. London: Routledge and Kegan Paul.

Ruether, R. R. (1983) *Sexism and God-talk: Toward a Feminist Theology*. Boston: Beacon Press.

Sedgwick, E. K. (1990) *Epistemology of the Closet*. Berkeley: University of California Press.

Sedgwick, E. K. (1991) How to bring your kids up gay. *Social Text, 29*, pp. 18–27.

Spelman, E. (1988) *Inessential Woman*. Boston: Beacon Press.

Stuart, E. (Ed.) (1997) *Religion is a Queer Thing*. London: Cassell.

Stuart, E. (2003) *Gay and Lesbian Theologies: Repetitions and Critical Difference*. Hampshire: Ashgate.

Thomas, C. (Ed.) (2000) *Straight with a Twist*. Urbana and Chicago: University of Illinois Press.

Walker, A. (1983) *In Search of Our Mothers' Gardens: Womanist Prose*. San Diego: Harcourt Brace Jovanovich.

Warner, M. (1993) *Fear of a Queer Planet*. Minneapolis: University of Minnesota Press.

Wittig, M. (1991) *The Straight Mind*. Boston: Beacon Press.

2

QUEERING 'TRADITIONAL' THEOLOGY

Feminist and gay and lesbian theologies were concerned with identity-based issues. This chapter begins by examining how queer theologies move beyond identity-based theologies. Then, considering the 'indecent theology' of Marcella Althaus-Reid, the chapter looks at queer theologies that destabilise God and Christ. Indecent theologies disrupt traditional interpretations in Christianity, including doctrine, rites, and rituals. At times, queer theologies have used philosophical reason to provide arguments as to why Christianity should make space for the inclusion of LGBTQ+ people. In theology these strategies are called apologetic strategies, and queer theologies to date have largely been focused on this area. This chapter briefly considers recent calls in queer theologies that suggest a move away from such apologetics (Tonstad, 2018). The chapter concludes with a consideration of Christian traditions through a queer lens, discussing queer worship and queer sacraments.

Queer theologies are not a synonym for lesbian and gay theologies. Queer theologies go beyond looking at sexuality. Elizabeth Stuart states:

> Queer theology, though it usually begins with issues of sexuality, is not really 'about' sexuality in the way that gay and lesbian theology is about sexuality. Queer theology is actually about theology. In gay and lesbian theology, sexuality interrogated theology; in queer theology, theology interrogates sexuality but from a different place than modern theology has traditionally done, the place of tradition (Stuart, 2003: 102–103).

Queer theologies, just like queer theory, move beyond queer identities. Instead of being identity-based and concerned with LGBTQ+ people, one of the insights from queer theologies is that they are anti-identity. Queer disrupts and rejects identity categories, so there is no such thing as a queer identity in any true sense. Of course, issues of sexuality can be examined through a queer lens, but the lens is open to anyone who wishes to use the critical insights of queer theory. That said, the experiences of gay and lesbian people, alongside other marginalised individuals, are very effective in showing the powerful, hegemonic structures in Christianity which require disruption.

Gerard Loughlin's essay, 'What is Queer? Theology after Identity' (2008), offers helpful inroads to understanding what queer theologies do (or undo!). In his opening comments he states, 'Theology is a queer thing. It has always been a queer thing' (Loughlin, 2008: 143). He points in two directions. First, he points to the queerness of theology, using the definition of 'queer' to mean strange or odd. Loughlin comments how theology is 'strange' as it 'does not fit into the modern world' (2008: 144). Second, he points to the task of *queering*, where Christian traditions and theologies are read through a queer filter. Queering is to use a queer lens to reinterpret texts and contexts. This enterprise uses imaginative and creative tools to ask 'what if …?' A queer reading therefore makes traditional readings unstable. Queer theologies deconstruct the building blocks of Christianity but may reshape the pieces in new, constructive ways.

As it is undefinable, like queer theory, it is more helpful to consider what queer theologies do, rather than are. Queer theologies disrupt any 'normal' or 'natural' readings of Christianity in its theological forms, including tradition, scripture, worship, fellowship, dogmas, and beliefs. Queer also removes binary thinking and presumptions, as we will see in the conception of Althaus-Reid's 'Queer God' below. Importantly, as Christianity operates on institutional levels through hierarchal church structures, queer theologies expose the power relations at play within the production of theology in the institutions of the Christian churches. Queer theologies interrogate institutional hierarchies and what have been considered sources of authority in theology, such as scripture and doctrines. The Christian tradition is undoubtedly patriarchal and heteronormative. Queer theologies therefore *re-write* and *right* Christianity to some extent. As expected, the production of queer theologies has sometimes been met with disinterest or dismissal from authoritative structures within church organisations and conservative Christians. There is a real tension between queer studies and Christianity, with suspicion on both sides. Althaus-Reid states how 'on the one side there are Christians who think that queer studies offend Christianity, while on the other there is a suspicion that a too close association with Christianity will contaminate queer studies' (Althaus-Reid, 2008: 107).

Susannah Cornwall observes 'a case of queer theory and Christianity speaking in different languages, where the language-game of Christianity [...] simply does not make sense to theorists who are not themselves grounded in it' (Cornwall, 2011: 236). The different languages represent the different positions of those whose work falls under the umbrella of queer theologies. There are Christian theologians who use a queer lens while remaining faithful to the building blocks and master narratives of the tradition. In theology, systematic theology formulates ordered and reasoned accounts of Christian doctrines, looking at what the Bible teaches or what is known and true about God. Queer theologians who work systematically have their starting points and positions in doctrine in Christian theology, and they uncover a queer interpretation or lens within it. Using the same idea of theologies as languages, Stuart says how this option is preferable, as focusing solely on contemporary, rational, critical thought was the downfall of gay and lesbian theology:

> Gay and lesbian theology made the mistake of putting its ultimate trust in the traditions of modernity rather than the traditions of Christianity with the result that it has sometimes ceased to be recognisable as theology at all, and forfeited its place in contemporary Christian dialogue because it no longer speaks the same language nor does it follow the same 'grammatical' rules as its opponents (Stuart, 2003: 105).

Another approach to queer theologies comes from the perspective that breaks free from the rules of Christianity, as queer ruptures regulation. Researchers and writers who are grounded in queer theory approach Christianity from a theoretical lens. Queer theologies can also be said to be produced in specific contexts or positions, often referred to as contextual theology. Isherwood and Althaus-Reid state that 'theology has always been contextual, and it has always depended on a theoretical framework of interpretation of the world' (Isherwood & Althaus-Reid, 2004: 4). Queer theologies in global contexts are further detailed in Chapter 3.

Queer theologies work in two ways, therefore. They show a continuation of systematic theology and a disruption of it. Althaus-Reid observes how queer theologies are an exercise of 'serious doubting' (Althaus-Reid, 2000: 5). In this she suggests that theologians should look at the theological methods that make traditional theologies indifferent to the reality of people's contexts. The power of traditional theology is found in such methods. It is the traditional methods of doing theology which are exclusive and exclusionary, so queer theologies re-examine and disrupt these methods.

There has also been concern around the engagement of queer theologies with queer theory. While their entrance on the academic stage was in sync with the popularity of queer theory, it has been noted that queer theologies do not always engage with the texts and critical analysis of queer theory. Cornwall notes this distinction and is concerned that 'if queer theologians do not use the term in the same way that queer critical theorists do, this may make queer theology less credible as an intellectual discourse' (Cornwall, 2011: 24).

INDECENT THEOLOGY

Marcella Althaus-Reid (1952–2009) was a Latin American liberation theologian and an eminent scholar in the field of queer theologies. She wore many hats as a theologian: feminist, liberationist, queer. Her prolific contributions to queer theologies are unparalleled and her death left a huge gap and questions for the future of queer theologies. Althaus-Reid's thought produced theologies that were completely disruptive and daring. Instead of relying on systematic order, Althaus-Reid relied on the senses and on action. Her queer theologies were passionate theologies of feeling and doing. She states that 'a Queer popular theology is an unruly one. It may bring some chaos and disorder to the effective ideology of Christian theology, but its contribution is immense' (Althaus-Reid, 2004b: 9). Her theology broke away from traditional, feminist, and liberation moulds.

A little detail about her own background provides the context for her theological projects. Althaus-Reid had left Argentina, completed her doctoral studies, and embarked on her research career in Scotland. Although some would say Althaus-Reid's theology is a cocktail of western and Latin American ingredients, her use of Latin American contexts ensures her theologies are grounded in the living experiences of Latin American people, as she tackles issues which are relevant and important to these contexts. Leopoldo Cervantes Ortiz states:

> Though she walked the path traveled many times by other Latin American theologians who studied in Europe, her theology was not merely an academic exercise, cold, calculated, and remote-controlled to a particular audience. To understand this, we must remember her work in Argentina and Scotland among underserved communities (Cervantes Ortiz, 2016: 29).

In 2000 Althaus-Reid released a text which would shake the foundations of theology. Her book *Indecent Theology* (2000) uncovers how all theology is sexual theology, 'based on sexual categories and heterosexual binary systems, obsessed with sexual behaviours and orders, every theological discourse is implicitly a sexual discourse, a decent one, an accepted one' (Althaus-Reid, 2000: 22). Her *Indecent Theology* was provocative, revolutionary, and sexually explicit. To glimpse at the radical nature of her theology, the book opens with a question about the poor women who sell lemons on the streets of her home town in Argentina. Althaus-Reid suggests that the women do not wear underwear while they work and claims that theologians who do not wear underwear are able to challenge the 'decent' theology which has been dominant. Althaus-Reid vividly describes their poverty, their business, their interactions, and their sex. She says, 'That is the point for a theology without underwear, made by people whose sexual misfortunes, personal or political, needed to be reflected upon as part of our theological praxis' (2000: 28).

Indecent Theology also raises problems around the image of Mary within Latin American religious culture, stating that Mary's status as a virgin means that the poor women of her area are unable to identify with her. Althaus-Reid describes poor women as rarely being virgins. She notes how it is not Mary the mother of Jesus who has become significant for theology, but the construct of Mary in the Christian tradition, who has become 'the religious alien Virgin' (Althaus-Reid, 2000: 72). Mary the mother of Jesus has been sanitised by the Christian tradition, and Althaus-Reid describes her as 'the rich white woman who does not walk' (Althaus-Reid, 2004b: 30).

Fully aware of her task of 'talking obscenities to theology' (Althaus-Reid, 2000: 87), she moves from a critique of the theological ideal of Mary to how Jesus has been constructed in theology. She states how Jesus 'has been dressed theologically as a heterosexually orientated (celibate) man. Jesus with erased genitalia; Jesus minus erotic body' (2000: 114). Heterosexual masculinity is presumed and attributed to Jesus. The fact that theology has rarely considered Jesus as a sexual being 'does not allow us to see his relationship with his community or with us as instances of the way that human beings relate to each other' (2000: 114). Because of this erasure of Jesus's sexuality within Christian theology, Althaus-Reid spots a gap and uses her imagination to plug it. She says it is possible that 'Jesus may have been a transvestite, a butch lesbian, a gay or a heterosexual person' (2000: 114). Althaus-Reid imagines a Bisexual Christ, a 'Bi/Christ', which allows Jesus to be cast outside of a heterosexual identity. In 2003 she released a further text, *The Queer God*, which built on these ideas.

The work of Althaus-Reid blazed a trail in queer theologies. She states how 'in theology it is not stability but a sense of discontinuity which is most valuable' (Althaus-Reid, 2000: 4). Demonstrating how the Christian tradition is unstable is a queer strategy. It only appears stable because people repeat it. Althaus-Reid was concerned with theologies from the margins that used the language of the centre. In order for theology to be truly radical it had to interrogate the centre from the margins. In *The Sexual Theologian* (2004), Isherwood and Althaus-Reid note how the position of queer theologies is at the margins:

> It is a theology from the margins which wants to remain at the margins [...] Terrible is the fate of theologies from the margin when they want to be accepted by the centre! Queer theology strives instead for differentiation and plurality [...] queer theology is a political and sexual

> queering of theology which goes beyond the gender paradigm of thinking of the early years of feminist theology but also transcends the fixed assumptions of gay and lesbian theology (Isherwood & Althaus-Reid, 2004: 3).

In seeking to theologise from the margins, Althaus-Reid places value on the importance of life narratives as a source for theology. An entire chapter in *Indecent Theology* is concerned with the 'theology of sexual stories'. She states, 'the everyday lives of people always provide us with a starting point for a process of doing contextual theology without exclusion' (Althaus-Reid, 2000: 4). Chapter 5 of this book explores the queer theologies which emerge from engaging with queer lives.

QUEERING GOD/CHRIST

> Then indecent theologians may say: 'God, the Faggot; God, the Drag Queen; God, the Lesbian. God, the heterosexual woman who does not accept the constructions of ideal heterosexuality; God, the ambivalent, not easily classified sexually' (Althaus-Reid, 2000: 95).

Althaus-Reid dared to imagine what God and Mary's sexuality would be. This was a substantial move from the discussion of human sexuality and sexual ethics within theology to the idea of divine sexuality. Human understanding of sexuality often means it is a taboo subject, better not discussed. Although we are surrounded with sexualised images, including in advertising and media, talking about sex is often seen as vulgar, dirty or indecent. Sex itself is messy. Therefore, imagining God as sexual moves away from the idea of God as sanitised, and this reveals a God to whom humans can relate because of their own experiences of being sexual. Imagining God as sexual is therefore an indecent task. Indecently, Althaus-Reid asks, 'is theology the art of putting your hands under the skirts of God?' (Althaus-Reid, 2004a: 99). She states, 'God is also queer: perhaps the first queer of all' (2004a: 103).

It becomes part of Althaus-Reid's theological tactic to use shock and indecency to queer traditional ideas of God. Queer theologies are boundaryless, indecent, sexual, and do not shy away from intimacy; after all, such intimacy is part of human life. Mainstream theology has previously excluded the poor and the marginalised, who have received little space or attention in dominant theologies. Althaus-Reid's conceptions of God and Mary provide images which are far removed from traditional imaginings. Indecent theology provides dialogue between sexual, embodied contexts and the Christian tradition.

In her 2003 publication, *The Queer God*, Althaus-Reid aims to envision God outside of heterosexuality and the traditional ideas of Christianity. The book engages in a theological queering, noting how heterosexuality has shaped understanding in theology. God and Christian theology must be liberated from heterosexuality, which has become a *straight*-jacket for Christianity. Taking God out of the closet liberates God; as Althaus-Reid states, 'Queering theology, the theological task and God is all part of a coming out of the closet for Christianity which is no longer simply the highroad of classical theology' (Althaus-Reid, 2003: 4).

To engage in queer theologies, Althaus-Reid states that the task requires an honesty from theologians themselves. She explains that 'God cannot be Queered unless theologians have the courage to come out from their homosexual, lesbian, bisexual, transgendered, transvestite or (ideal) heterosexual closets. Out-of-the-closet theologians do not leave the personal aside' (Althaus-Reid, 2000: 88). Queer theologians, therefore, offer information about themselves and their background. This allows for their position and agenda to be explicit. Honesty in the production of theology means that queer theologies do not pretend to be neutral or universal.

For Althaus-Reid, queer theologies wrestle with the idea of the God of the centre. Her conception of the Queer God reflects her allegiance to liberation theologies. The Queer God is 'the stranger at the gate of churches and theology [...] God is a truly marginal God [...] the Queer God is the God who went into exile with God's people and remained there in exile with them' (Althaus-Reid, 2004b: 146). Of course, conceptualising God is a human activity, and this is one area which denotes the limitations of human capacity to think about God. Both Elizabeth Stuart and Althaus-Reid state how contextual theologies may fall into a tendency to create a mirror-God (Stuart, 2003: 29; Althaus-Reid, 2003: 52). Yet imagining God in these ways is a corruption of the methods of theology, and, according to Althaus-Reid, queer theologies must 'move objects and subjects of theology around, turning points of reference and re-positioning bodies of knowledge and revelation in sometimes unsuitable ways' (Althaus-Reid, 2003: 52).

Returning to queer concepts of God, Gerard Loughlin works within the tradition and points to Thomas Aquinas's idea of negative theology. Negative theology explores the nature of what God is not, as humans are unable to state exactly what God is. Loughlin therefore works from inside the writings of traditional theology to discuss the nature of God as queer. Following Aquinas, Loughlin states 'the most that we can say about God is that God *is* [...] In an analogous way we can say that queer *is*, even if we cannot say in what queer consists other than by pointing to the effects of its deployment' (Loughlin, 2007: 10). He claims that the idea of queer is similar to the idea of God – that it defies definition: 'queer might be offered as a name for God' (2007: 10).

Elsewhere, Patrick Cheng's *An Introduction to Queer Theology: Radical Love* focuses on the concept of God as 'radical love' (Cheng, 2011: 50). This radical love 'breaks down fixed categories and boundaries' (2011: 51). For Cheng, the Trinity is imagined as an 'internal community of radical love' (2011: 56); Jesus 'the embodiment of radical love' (2011: 78); and Mary the 'bearer of radical love' (2011: 87). Cheng works within the Christian tradition with a confessional yet queer lens by upholding the themes of Christian theology to shape his queer reading. In this the creeds and Christian theological concepts such as sin, grace, atonement, and the sacraments provide a framework for Cheng's discussion of radical love.

QUEER TRADITION

There are a number of queer theologies that state how Christianity has always been queer, and to cover the range of discussions is impossible in this short space. I suggest that readers interested in this specific area should engage with suggested texts described in the further reading section, particularly Loughlin (2007). Among these thinkers is Stuart, who asserts that 'Christian theology was queer two thousand years before queer theory was invented' (Stuart, 2003: 102). Stuart is referring to the fact that Christianity is a religion which focuses on and displaces bodies. The virgin birth, the Body of Christ as a metaphor for the church, the death of Christ through crucifixion, and the act of remembering Christ's body through the Eucharist are all examples of how theologians are able to reflect on the main beliefs of the Christian tradition and examine how they are already queer or subversive. In this there is a suggestion that the tradition was queer long before queer theory.

By adopting this strategy some theologians use what I refer to as a 'queer-view mirror'. Like a rear-view mirror they reflect back on the tradition and re-examine it from the lens of the present. It is a task which looks retrospectively on the tradition with the theories and knowledge of today. Obviously 'queer' did not exist throughout the 2,000 years of Christianity, as it is a contemporary concept. Yet there are multiple examples of queer readings of non-normative gender and sexuality within the tradition, perhaps without the current terminology we have today to label them as such. The queer-view mirror provides a creative, critical, and analytical lens to offer queer readings of the tradition. Yet queering elements of the tradition is not enough for Jeremy Carrette. He states that, for Christianity to become truly queer, it has to queer its foundations, including its belief in one God and its exclusive possession of truth. Carrette states, 'we now need to rewrite the history of Christian theology' (Carrette, 2001: 297).

Queering the tradition has often involved queer readings of the lives and work of the early church fathers or saints. Latin American theologian Martín Hugo Córdova Quero states, 'to queer the past implies to ask different questions of it [...] attempting to find answers that go beyond what has traditionally been accepted' (Córdova Quero, 2004: 26). In an example of using a queer-view mirror, Córdova Quero re-examines the life of Aelred of Rievaulx, the English medieval monk. First, he re-examines the relationship of Aelred with a fellow monk, Simon. Following Simon's death, Aelred writes a lament of grief for his beloved friend. This lament is interpreted as an expression of both brotherly and erotic love between Aelred and Simon. Aelred developed a theology of friendship, and he allowed the monks in his monastery to express their feelings physically, thereby removing feelings of guilt, sin, and shame associated with the body and same-sex physical contact with others. Córdova Quero's analysis of social orders during the period in which Aelred lived reveals how monasteries were 'where males engaged in homoerotic practices gathered, [monasteries] were places in which alternatives could be explored' (2004: 42).

It is not just the church fathers who are examined through this queer-view mirror. Elsewhere, Córdova Quero offers a queer reading of Mary of Magdala (Córdova Quero, 2006), exposing how Christians had trapped her in binary thinking, as a sinner or a saint. Mary represents a break in the decent story of Christianity, and Córdova Quero's examination demonstrates how Mary of Magdala went from being depicted as a sinful woman to a virtuous leader of the early church. In tracing the queerness of the treatment of Mary Magdalene and using a metaphor of 'indecent theology' borrowed from Althaus-Reid, Córdova Quero concludes that 'every *theology* is, in fact, *ideology*; ultimately there is no such thing as *innocent theology*' (2006: 82).

Within the edited volume *Queer Theology: Rethinking the Western Body* (Loughlin, 2007) there is a whole section of rich examples of queer/ing tradition. Again, the method of using a queer-view mirror helps to re-examine traditional concepts, and the volume details further queer examinations. For example, the early church father Gregory of Nyssa has been reinterpreted by Virginia Burrus. She examines the notion of desire in the theology of Gregory, analysing concepts of virginity, marriage, and fatherhood. Amy Hollywood provides a critical reading of medieval women, offering a queer reading of three mystic women – Mechthild of Magdeburg, Hadewijch of Anvers, and Marguerite Porete. Their devotion in worship is revealed as sacred eroticism, and the language of their mystical writings challenges assumptions of gender. Similarly, Christopher Hinkle offers a queer reading of Saint John of the Cross. In resisting the temptation to read John as a gay saint, as other theologians have tended to do, Hinkle examines John's submission to the dominant God as an act of burning desire and love.

Queer theologies are not always written or text based. Other examples of queering the tradition are found in forms of queer art. Kittredge Cherry's *Art That Dares* (2007) offers dramatic new visions of a woman Christ, a gay Jesus, and saints in love. In Cherry's rich anthology, various artists are incorporated into a collection of paintings, photographs, and sculpture which offer new artistic forms for spiritual and personal contemplation. The paintings include Alex Donis's images of Jesus and Lord Rama from Hindu mythology kissing passionately (Cherry, 2007: 36). The theme of kissing continues with a gay embrace depicted in the Judas Kiss by Becki Jayne Harrelson (2007: 42) and a passionate kiss between Mary Magdalene and the Virgen de Guadalupe (2007: 39, private artist). In photographic form, the work of Elisabeth Ohlson Wallin depicts an image of Jesus entitled 'Sermon on the Mount', where he is surrounded by half-naked leather-clad men wearing chains and restraints (2007: 74). Ohlson Wallin's work continues in her reimaging the iconic 'Pietà', where Mary is cradling the dead body of Jesus; in Ohlson Wallin's queer reconceptualisation of the piece she uses a gay man dying of AIDS in a hospital ward being cradled by a woman in blue.

Queer images are used to reflect upon and speak back to queer lives. Cherry states how 'the images are arising now because the conventional Jesus is no longer adequate' (Cherry, 2007: 8). Throughout the history of Judaism and Christianity there has always been a charge of blasphemy against those who make images of idols and icons. Within the Hebrew Bible/Old Testament, one of God's commandments to Moses was against creating images of God: 'You shall not make for yourself an image in the form of anything in heaven above or on the earth beneath or in the waters below' (Exodus, 20: 4). Some Christian denominations do use images as a focus for worship, yet Cherry is keen to point out that there are power structures at play with religious images. She states, 'by controlling religious images, they control people […] unauthorized images can be made by unauthorized people' (Cherry, 2007: 9). Examples of the art work from Cherry's collections are suggested in the online resources section at the end of this chapter.

BEYOND APOLOGETIC STRATEGIES

In the study of theology, apologetics does not mean apologising for one's faith. The term comes from the Greek: 'apologia' meaning a 'reasoned defence'. Therefore, traditional apologetics is the defence of Christian religious doctrines through reasoned arguments. In terms of gender and sexuality, apologetic strategies may examine theological questions relating to gender transitioning or same-sex marriage. Queer theologians who engage in apologetics look for ways to counter claims that Christianity is incompatible with LGBTQ+ identities. They may look to doctrines and to the Bible to find examples within the Christian message that appeal to queer imaginations. Gay and lesbian and queer theologies have largely been done using apologetic strategies.

In *Queer Theology: Beyond Apologetics,* Linn Tonstad is of the position that 'queer theology is not about apologetics, or at least that it *should* not be about apologetics' (Tonstad, 2018: 16). She states that 'Christians should stop arguing over issues of sexual morality altogether, and instead should allow the discernment of the individual conscience before God to rule' (2018: 38). Tonstad states how the focus of the queer project in theology is capitalism – the relationship between the economy and sex. She describes how heterosexual marriage, monogamy, and reproduction are the cogs of capitalism. 'Children are needed for the continuance and growth of capitalism: they must be born, clothed, fed, and educated, so that they, in turn, become productive workers and consumers' (2018: 81). Religion has sanctified this process, giving it 'an aura of holiness, divine will and ethical responsibility' (2018: 82).

In stating her own position, she says 'I am a Christian theologian who works in queer theory as well. Many Christian theologians and many queer theorists believe that combination is possible. Those who think such a combination is possible often disagree about how such a task should be undertaken' (2018: 50). She reiterates her claim that queer apologetics offers little theological value and acknowledges that her own work could be assessed as being too 'doctrine-heavy than most theologians would prefer' (2018: 50).

Queer cannot be pinned down. The plural term, queer theologies, is therefore much more appropriate in highlighting the different languages spoken by queer theologians, who all hold their own preferences for methods and allegiances. Queer is indefinable and unfixable. Therefore, queer theologians should exercise caution when stating what queer theologies should or should not be about, as this can be seen as an attempt to carve out a normativity. Whether apologetic strategies are used or not, queer theologies are committed to the task of disruption, removing power structures and hierarchies, and demonstrating the instability of firmly fixed objects and positions. Queer theologies are diverse and plural. Queer theologies are multiple and varied, their richness allows them to speak differently.

One of the major themes which characterise what queer theologies do is the idea of continuity and disruption of traditional theology. Queer theologies refuse to allow a patriarchal and heteronormative tradition to continue without being examined, critiqued, subverted, and disrupted. The Christian tradition, therefore, only seems stable because it has been repeated throughout the centuries, and that repetition has firmed up its hold on power structures which regulate theologies, bodies, and beliefs. Elsewhere I call this 'Christian-normativity' (Greenough, 2018: 172). A resistance to repeating traditional Christianity is the task of queer theologies; as Althaus-Reid states, 'queer traditions are made of strange alliances of memories of discontinuity and disorder, shared by communities of people with pride and resistance' (Althaus-Reid, 2003: 10). Attention now turns to the communities of Christians as a body, where Christian worship is queer and queered.

QUEER WORSHIP

Queer people are not outsiders to the church. Christianity has not only always had queer members, has not only always had the potential to be queered, but has from the start been a site of radical queerness (Larrimore, 2015: 2).

Mark Larrimore demonstrates how there have always been queer members in churches, and is in agreement with theologians like Stuart who claim that Christianity has always been queer. There are a number of questions that have become popular which relate to the inclusion of LGBTQ+ people within the churches. Why do people who are LGBTQ+ remain within the churches, whose positional statements are often homophobic and transphobic? How does someone reconcile being Christian with other non-normative aspects of their identity? In Chapter 5 I address some of these questions when looking at queer theologies that emerge from queer Christian lives. In this section on queer worship I consider the important developments within Christian denominations to include marginalised people. Then I consider how Christian worship can be seen to reflect the lives of queer people. In examining queer worship we look from two perspectives: the first reflects on the elements and relevance of worship for 'queer' people; the second reveals elements of Christian worship which are unusual, or queer.

The vast majority of Christian denominations have seen a development of affiliated gay and lesbian or LGBTQ+ organisations. Examples include but are not limited to Roman Catholics (Quest), the Episcopalians (Integrity), Methodists (Affirmation), the Association of Welcoming and Affirming Baptists, the Gay Salvationist Support Group, and Evangelicals Concerned. An increasing number of churches are making it known publicly that they are welcoming, open, and affirming, despite the positions of their institutional hierarchies. There are a number of LGBTQ+ friendly worship organisations and churches across the world whose worship is designed to affirm the beliefs and identities of LGBTQ+ Christians. The Metropolitan Community Church (MCC) is an example of a church community that ministers specifically to LGBTQ+ people. The church was founded in California a year before the Stonewall riots by the Rev. Troy Perry. According to their organisational website, today there are 43,000 members and adherents in almost 300 congregations in 22 countries.[1] In addition to a presence of MCC churches in Australasia, Europe, and North America, there are also ministries within Africa (including Kenya and Nigeria) and Latin America. There is a named presence in Russia, where recent legal reforms allow penalties against homosexual propaganda. In Asia, important efforts in relation to LGBTQ+ inclusion and queer theologies in Christian religious communities are noted in, for example, the Jakarta Theological Seminary in Indonesia, the National Council of Churches and the United Theological College in India, MCC churches in the Philippines, Tong Kwang church in Taiwan, and Blessed Ministry Community Church and the Queer Theology Academy in Hong Kong.

In his discussion on 'queer-church', Andy Braunston details his own experiences as a founding and senior pastor of a MCC congregation in the UK. Braunston notes how queer worship is able to self-fashion and create what church is by refusing to play by the rules of mainstream churches. This has been empowering and attractive to those who have left traditional congregations. Braunston details what queer-church and queer worship looks like:

> The thing that unites us is the feeling that we are making the rules for
> ourselves. We can make our own liturgies and ceremonies which mark
> our lives and loves [...] Our poets and musicians are now writing
> hymns for us [...] We are re-creating the church in a way which is
> powerful and meaningful to our loves and lives (Braunston, 1997: 102).

In Christian theology, liturgy is a form of public worship which
can include rites, rituals, ceremonies, and sacraments. Specific suggestions for queer liturgy come from the authors of *Religion is a
Queer Thing* (Stuart, 1997). There are practical suggestions
throughout the text, including exercises and reflections for use as
part of worship services. The span of themes is wide, with due care
and attention to make the language accessible in discussions of the
Bible, God, the queer Christ, salvation, liturgy, and queer ethics.
The editor, Elizabeth Stuart, is keen to include lesbian, gay,
bisexual, and transgender voices in the design of queer worship.
She says, 'only if queer theology reflects the reality and spirituality
of those who live the reality of queer lives in the mess and muddle
of the world will queer theology [have] the potential to transform
not just queer people but all men and women' (1997: 4).

In a similar vein to Stuart, Martin Stringer advocates that we
embrace our messy bodies and lives as a part of worship. He is
among scholars who note how Christianity has been queer, revealed
in his reading of mainstream Anglican/Catholic worship as camp
and drag (Stringer, 2000). Stringer observes how worship is a physical and sensory experience, and focusing on these elements coun-
ters the discussions of worship as intellectual or spiritual, as he brings
the body back into focus. Indeed, Stringer points out how bodies
are integral to worship: the body of Christ and the liturgical body
are both widely discussed in theology, but these discussions are dis-
tanced from 'any real bodies, and particularly from any kind of
"bodily functions"' (2000: 38). The body is therefore idealised and
the realities of human bodies are avoided. Any part of the human
body that is functional, unclean, sinful or sexual is completely
ignored in discussions of the body in worship, according to Stringer.
In highlighting the camp aspects of worship, Stringer draws on parallels with drag, noting how the church sacristy is an all-male
environment in which men who are about to perform adorn
themselves in lace and jewels. Yet this playful reading is serious; as

Stringer concludes, 'if we are able, however, to move beyond the camp and to find alternative ways of expressing much more openly and directly our sexual selves in worship, then there may be much more hope and much more cause for rejoicing' (2000: 54).

Queer people are part of churches and worshipping communities. Siobhan Garrigan questions how significant life events in the lives of LGBTQ+ people are marked and celebrated within churches. She imagines coming-out services, re-naming ceremonies, house blessings, and blessings of same-sex unions (Garrigan, 2009: 213). Likewise, she asks 'how many times have you heard sermons in which the stories told are about LGBT people's lives?' (2009: 214). Garrigan calls for such rites to be part of whole services, rather than private and supplementary to public liturgical worship. By making something a private event, it hides its status from the community. In making this observation, Garrigan points to the fact that queer theologies have to be practical, rather than a theory or ideology when it comes to worship. In highlighting how worship, like theology, is gendered and heteronormative, Garrigan states how worship is truly queer when masculine references to God are removed. She states, 'queer worship is at its most controversial not when it proposes the acceptability of people coming to worship dressed in leather but when it suggests calling God something other than Father' (2009: 219). Just as feminist theology held concerns about the masculine language for God, within queer theologies descriptions of God reflect the preferred terminology from the worshipper.

In this sense we come to one of the most contested issues within the field: the relationship between queer-identities (LGBTQ+) and queer which serves as a rupture of identities. If queer disrupts identity, how can it be supposed to represent or support queer identities? There is often a blur between identity-informed queer theologies and queer theologies beyond identity.

To respond to this difficult question we must recall how queer theologies are not universal and not all theologians speak the same language. For some, queer theologies are intellectual and theoretical (queerly rupturing identities), while for others they are practical (serving queer identities). Queer theologies seem to be doing two different things. In one sense they seem to be working from a top-down approach grounded in theory, tradition, and reason; while, on the other hand, they work from a bottom-up approach grounded in the lives of queer people. Within each approach there are questions which are complex and challenging and this can lead to vagueness, or to disagreements between both approaches. Remember that queer theory serves to muddy the waters, so, as an academic area and approach, the waters will always be unclear and choppy. Queer allows for disciplinary promiscuity in a variety of approaches.

Inclusion in queer worshipping communities remains a significant issue on a practical level where LGBTQ+ people are able to choose to worship with others, including friends and family, in their local communities. The question of inclusion remains an important challenge to Christianity, despite theoretical or reasoned positions, precisely because of the emotional toil in the daily lives of those who are LGBTQ+ and Christian. Negotiating what can be seen as conflicting identities is a long, difficult, and emotional process: individuals may choose to reject the centre of mainstream theology on a personal level, while some wish to remain. In blending queer and practical theologies, these discussions are important to LGBTQ+ Christians.

Abandonment, rejection or isolation from religious communities feature in the lives of queer Christians. The loss of the worship community can be significant. Deryn Guest notes that there is a real loss when the religious community one has grown up in becomes a thing of the past. On leaving the Salvation Army, Guest recalls experiences of loss and grief:

> what I had not anticipated was the sheer enormity of loss that this action entailed: loss of a religious home akin to a much loved family of would-be aunts, uncles, nieces, nephews, cousins, grandparents; loss of its liturgical environments – particularly in musical and lyrical heritage, which for all its gendered stereotypes and heteronormativity, had always held profound significance for me; and the loss of relationship with God (Guest, 2008: 202).

Religious identities are often constructed from birth, through relationships with individuals in local worship communities and surroundings. For LGBTQ+ Christians, therefore, the question of inclusion remains a significant one.

QUEER SACRAMENTS

> Queer theologies do not disregard church traditions. However, the pro-
> cess of queering may turn them upside down (Althaus-Reid, 2003: 8).

Althaus-Reid notes how the active agenda of queering Christian
traditions is disruptive. In this way, Stuart has offered comprehensive queer readings of the sacraments (Stuart, 1997, 2007, 2010).
The underlying principle of her scholarship is that 'The body of
Christ is queer. That body is made available to Christians through
the sacraments' (Stuart, 2007: 66). Within Christianity, sacraments
are significant rites of passage, bringing Christians closer to God.
Within the Catholic and Orthodox traditions there are seven
major sacraments: baptism, Eucharist, confirmation, reconciliation,
marriage, anointing of the sick, and holy orders. The Protestant
view rejects five of the sacraments above, citing baptism and
Eucharist as the only two important ones. In this overview of
queer sacraments I examine baptism and Eucharist as queer
sacraments. I also draw attention to the controversies surrounding
the marriage debate within Christian churches. Moreover, I
consider how there is a non-sacramental rite of passage which can
be considered queer: the concept of 'coming out'.

BAPTISM

A queer reading of baptism reveals it as a sacrament which moves
Christians beyond identity. Baptism is a sacrament of initiation: it is
a rite of naming an individual and their belonging to their church.
In some denominations, baptism is done to babies a few weeks
after their birth. In others, baptism is a choice a Christian makes as
an adult to become a full church member through their own free
will. At their baptism, Christians believe that their sins are washed
away. This is why water is an important sign of baptism. Christians
therefore die to sin. In a queer reading of the sacrament of baptism,
Stuart views baptism as the acquisition of a new identity, one that
surpasses human markers of identity. Stuart reveals how baptism
involves two simultaneous deaths: one to sin and the other to
identity. She states how baptism 'reveals the inadequacy of all other
forms of identity and the desire caught up in them' (Stuart, 2007:

67). Stuart's understanding of baptism is grounded in Paul's letter to the Galatians in the New Testament, where he declares: 'There is neither Jew nor Gentile, neither slave nor free, nor is there male and female, for you are all one in Christ Jesus' (3: 28). For Stuart, baptism signifies taking on a new identity as Christian, one which erases categories of identity that can separate people on earth. This belief is truly realised in the afterlife. In Christian theology, eschatology is the examination of death, judgement, and afterlife. Stuart's belief is that baptism is wholly connected to the eschatological promises stated by Paul in his letter to the Galatians. She notes how the promise of eternal afterlife makes those who are baptised 'people who in their own beings carry around with them the death that society fears' (Stuart, 2007: 73). Stuart claims that queer flesh is sacramental flesh. Through baptism, she states, 'in Christ maleness and femaleness and gay and straight are categories that dissolve before the throne of grace where only the garment of baptism remains' (2007: 75).

This idea of identity erasure is considered idealistic by some. Andy Buechal finds Stuart's reading of the sacrament 'rich and compelling, but also troubling in its idealism' (Buechal, 2015: 58). He states how Stuart's notion of baptism is grounded in what happens in the afterlife, rather than what happens currently on earth. According to Buechal, Stuart's reading means that 'no longer do we relate to one another as men and women, gay and straight, or via any other human identity' (2015: 63). He responds by stating that 'it is quite obvious that Christians are still bound up in the same cultural identities as anyone who is non-baptised. In fact, it is often the non-baptised who are more successful at exposing the non-ultimacy of these identities' (2015: 63). He notes how baptism is problematic for queer Christians, especially as the promises of being included into a Christian family often prove to be false. Buechal expresses this as follows:

> the baptized are not granted some special privilege that allows them to avoid the same cultural constructions, negotiations, and maneuvers as anyone else. In fact, if we look at the controversies over sex and gender in the churches, we would be led to believe the exact opposite (Buechal, 2015: 65).

For Buechal, the need for Christians to wait for the afterlife for issues of identity to be fixed, as Stuart suggests, is a step too far. He states that 'appeals to eschatology […] may not attend enough to questions that need to be addressed in the here and now' (Buechal, 2015: 73).

Beyond issues of identity, the links between birth and baptism are problematic too. Althaus-Reid is concerned with baptism as a rite which does not recognise, appreciate or celebrate the human nature of an individual. In fact, she states that it does the opposite, as it is 'a liturgical act based on a theology which devalues the human, in the sense that it assumes the incompleteness of the new-born human. However, it is also a devaluation of women, as if women are incapable of giving birth to children accepted by society as fully human' (Althaus-Reid, 2003: 136). Simply put, the explicit need for baptism undermines the human experience of birth. The performance of baptism in Christianity is seen as superior to birth, as baptism implies that humans are not part of the Christian family until they experience this rite. Althaus-Reid also stresses that this devaluing of humans extends to birth mothers, as they are rendered incapable of giving birth to children who are not accepted as fully human or complete until they are baptised. She concludes that 'baptism appears here as a sacramental supplement to birth' (2003: 136).

EUCHARIST

In Christian theology the Eucharist is a sacrament which recalls Jesus's actions at the Last Supper. For Catholics it is called the Blessed Sacrament, as Catholics believe in transubstantiation. Transubstantiation is the belief that, through the blessing of the priest, bread and wine are transformed into the actual body and blood of Jesus. Because of this idea, a queer reading of the Eucharist brings into play ideas about bodies and blood. Such ideas relate to human embodiments and human experiences. The union of Christ and Christian in the Eucharist can be seen as a fusion of bodies, using images which are shaped by sexual ideas. The sexual imagery of intimate experiences through the Eucharist is developed by Robert Goss in his essay 'Passionate Love for Christ: Out of the

Closet, Into the Streets' (Goss, 2000). Goss writes that, in celebrating the sacrament of the Eucharist, 'I envisioned making love
to Jesus, felt myself become sexually aroused, and climaxed in an
orgasmic union with Jesus the Christ [...] Jesus was my gay lover'
(2000: 300–301). Goss continues to describe the presence of Christ
in his lovemaking with his partner, Frank: 'Our sex was Euchar-
istic, intensely passionate, and intensely spiritual. During passionate
lovemaking, I felt Christ in a way that I only experienced in my
solitary erotic prayer. I felt Christ in our lovemaking and did not
want to give it up' (2000: 301). Stuart too agrees that 'God is in
there, rustling between the sheets, disrupting and dislocating'
(Stuart, 2010: 114), but for Stuart the satisfaction of experiencing
God's presence during a sexual encounter is only temporary. Stuart
warns that 'condensing God to human relating, whether in bed or
not, is dangerous because human relationships simply cannot bear
the weight of the divine' (2010: 114). Her queer Eucharist shows
how the diversity of human characteristics and identities are part of
the body of Christ:

> The chief characteristic of this body is its extraordinary diversity – all
> sexes, sexualities, races, classes are part of it, the decent and the
> indecent. The body of Christ in which our individual bodies find their
> meaning is the perfect queer community (Stuart, 2010: 122).

In another queer reading, Althaus-Reid stresses the physical aspect
of consuming divine flesh in the Eucharist. She labels the Eucharist
as a cannibalistic event, noting how the human consumption of
Christ's body and blood is both silent yet integral to Catholics. She
highlights the 'cannibalistic elements of eucharists, elegantly sup-
pressed and represented in theology' (Althaus-Reid, 2000: 57).

MARRIAGE

There is some unease in the discussion of the sacrament of marriage as it draws attention to the complex and antagonistic positions of the churches in recognising the loving relationships and
unions between same-sex couples. This discussion is expanded in
Chapter 5. Stuart sees the position of the churches as an almost
failing of LGBTQ+ people in allowing full membership to the

sacraments; as she states, 'the church's refusal to incorporate lesbian and gay and transsexual people into marriage demonstrates a lack of engagement with the eschatological and Christological dimension of the sacrament' (Stuart, 2007: 73).

The main Christian denominations, at the time of writing, still conceptualise marriage as the union between one man and one woman, with an understanding that the marriage will be sexually consummated and result in procreation. As a sacrament it is not difficult to see why a queer reading of marriage has been important for non-heterosexual identifying individuals. Moreover, it raises questions beyond same-sex discussions. What about relationships that extend beyond two people, where the relationship may include other partners? The principle of procreation is also inherently troubling for individuals who may choose not to have children or are unable to have children. How does adoption fit into the sense of marriage procreation? Susannah Cornwall offers an extensive discussion of these issues in *Un/Familiar Theology* (2017). Her un/familiar theology takes root in assessing the familiar concepts of the theological tradition, marriage and reproduction, before highlighting the complexity of social lived experiences which may be termed as 'unfamiliar' to the Christian tradition. Yet these experiences are 'precisely part of what the tradition may be yet to embrace. The unfamiliar is therefore both already a part of the tradition, and part of what the tradition may become' (Cornwall, 2017: 15). She balances the positions of those wishing to preserve the tradition by pointing out the reality of the lives of many in it. To some extent the tradition is not stable and unchanging in any case, and on these issues it must engage and evolve. She states:

> if same-sex marriage, for example, somewhat changes marriage, and adoptive parenting by same-sex couples or single people, for example, somewhat alters what we understand family and parenthood to be, this is not a departure to be mourned but a shift to be critically engaged (Cornwall, 2017: 2).

Cornwall is bold in her examination of marriage, reminding us that 'Christians do not own marriage' (Cornwall, 2017: 45) and that 'God did not invent marriage. Humans invented marriage, and humans can and do reinvent it too' (2017: 46).

Just as the Eucharist depicts a physical relationship with the body of Christ and Christians, there has been a marriage metaphor which emerges from a study of the relationship between God and Israel within the Hebrew Bible/Old Testament. This idea of God in a relationship with his people is reinterpreted by Christians in the concept of Jesus and the church. Loughlin recalls the story in John's gospel of the wedding at Cana, highlighting how we do not know who got married. The story is popular for recalling the miracle of Jesus turning water into wine, but Loughlin reconsiders the story, suggesting how Christ was marrying his disciple, John. He notes how this is a 'queer kind of marriage: the bonding of men in matrimony' (Loughlin, 2007: 2).

Sexual expression cannot solely be about reproduction, as traditional theologies hold. Goss notes how equating marriage with procreative sexuality denies it the pleasures of intimacy. Goss uncovers how the churches' attempt to regulate sexuality is a form of an expression of its power, and any attempt to subvert traditional marriage or promote sex for pleasure becomes a threat. Goss notes how these threats to marriage and family structures 'open the social construction of sexuality to innovative meanings and values' (Goss, 1993: 136). Moreover, by uncovering the social structures of sexuality and gender, Goss sees same-sex unions as free from patriarchy and heteronormative assumptions. He states, 'same sex unions are frequently without heterosexist power relations or conjugal stereotypes that are socially incorporated into the institute of marriage' (1993: 137). According to Goss, rather than recognising the union of same-sex partners, theology can learn from their relationships.

As marriage is a public event, with bans being read and celebrations with close friends and families, Cheng points to how this is an affirmation which has similarities to the experience of 'coming out'. He says 'the sacrament of matrimony is also closely connected with coming out because coming out is precisely what makes same-sex marriages possible in the first place' (Cheng, 2011: 124). As a pivotal event unique to the lives of LGBTQ+ people, coming out has its own ritual and transformation. Coming out is a queer sacrament.

COMING OUT AS SACRAMENT

The hostile positions from some churches towards LGBTQ+ people show how some individuals have been excluded from the sacraments. Chris Glaser discusses the effects of this on the lives of LGBTQ+ people:

> We have experienced word and sacrament not as open hands reaching to welcome us but as spiritually abusive fists ready to pummel us, not as open arms ready to embrace us but as intimidating arms pushing us away, protectively shielding rather than openly sharing the Body of Christ, the church (Glaser, 1998: 5).

Glaser argues that 'coming out' is the most important sacrament for LGBTQ+ people. It is important to note how the process of coming out as an act of self-affirmation is the total opposite of being 'outed', where an individual has no control or say in the disclosure. Glaser sees the act of coming out as spiritual; as he states, '*Coming out* is our unique sacrament, a rite of vulnerability that reveals the sacred in our lives – our worth, our love, our love-making, our beloved, our communities, our context of meaning, and our God' (Glaser, 1998: 9). He highlights the role that communities play in the rituals of the sacraments, because any enactment of the sacraments involves more than an individual but involves a whole community. Glaser states, 'just as the sacred nature of a sacrament cannot be forced on anyone who does not believe in its efficacy, coming out requires the cooperation and belief of those affected' (1998: 9–10). He sees how the act of coming out echoes each of the traditional sacraments. For example, Glaser notes how in baptism Christians die to their old lives, and the act of coming out mirrors this death, as LGBTQ+ people are able to live a more authentic life and become part of a new community. Glaser describes how coming out reflects the nature of the Eucharist, as the celebration of the sacrament recalls the vulnerability and sacrifice of Jesus and how this leads to union with God.

CONCLUSION

This chapter has provided a basic overview of scholarship in the area of queer theologies. Alternative conceptions of God, Christ, and Christian traditions are revealed using a queer lens to re-examine traditional theology. These alternatives disrupt traditional theologies.

Queer theologies are also able to serve the marginalised, who can locate their own identifications and experiences within the Christian story. Moreover, queer theologies release ideas of God and Christ from heteronormative and patriarchal assumptions. On a practical level this chapter has engaged with the concept of queer worship and queer Christian life through the sacraments. What emerges within the production of queer theologies is the problem with the word 'queer'. Queer theologies can be seen to contradict themselves as they function in two ways. They aim to disrupt categories of identity, yet queer theologies have been seen as attempting to advocate for the representation and inclusion of LGBTQ+ identities in Christianity. In many respects, queer theologies *queer* themselves because of this tension between both applications! They undo one another. The next chapter offers further insights into the plurality and diversity of queer theologies in global contexts.

FURTHER READING AND ONLINE RESOURCES

Althaus-Reid, M. (2000) *Indecent Theology*. London: Routledge.

Althaus-Reid reveals how theology is a sexual act. She calls for a theology which is committed to social justice and transformation of the powerful structures in theology and in society.

Cheng, P. S. (2011) *Radical Love: An Introduction to Queer Theology*. New York: Seabury Books.

Cheng offers an overview of queer theology, examining the role of God, Jesus, and the Holy Spirit. He provides discussion of the sacraments through a queer lens, as well as a comprehensive reference list for those looking for further reading on the subject of same-sex marriage (p.123, footnote 68).

Loughlin, G. (Ed.) (2007) *Queer Theology: Rethinking the Western Body*. London: Blackwell.

A collection of academic essays exploring queer theologies in the west. The essays particularly offer theological reflections on Christian church, history, and tradition.

Stuart, E. (Ed.) (1997) *Religion is a Queer Thing*. London: Cassell.

An overview of Christian faith for LGBTQ+ people. The book offers accessible insights, particularly to those working within ministry or church communities, as well as offering practical ideas for worship.

Tonstad, L. (2018) *Queer Theology. Beyond Apologetics.* Eugene: Wipf and Stock.

Tonstad details how queer theologies should no longer be about apologetic strategies. She considers what apologetic strategies look like and why they do not satisfy, before considering how queer theology is connected more widely to capitalism.

http://qspirit.net/blog/

This website looks at queer readings of Christianity, transforming biblical stories and saints into queer works of art. The blog also has an up-to-date list of books and key concepts in queer theology.

NOTE

1   https://www.mccchurch.org/overview/history-of-mcc/

REFERENCES

Althaus-Reid, M. (2000) *Indecent Theology*. London: Routledge.
Althaus-Reid, M. (2003) *The Queer God*. London: Routledge.
Althaus-Reid, M. (2004a) 'Queer I Stand: Lifting the Skirts of God', in Althaus-Reid, M. and Isherwood, L. (Eds), *The Sexual Theologian*, pp. 99–109. London: Continuum.
Althaus-Reid, M. (2004b) *From Feminist to Indecent Theology*. London: SCM Press.
Althaus-Reid, M. (2008) 'The Bi/girl Writings: From Feminist Theology to Queer Theologies', in Isherwood, L. and McPhillips, K. (Eds.) *Post-Christian Feminisms: A Critical Approach*, pp. 105–116. Aldershot: Ashgate.
Braunston, A. (1997) 'The Church', in Stuart, E. (Ed.) *Religion is a Queer Thing*, pp. 96–104. London: Cassell.
Buechal, A. (2015) *That We Might Become God*. Eugene: Cascade Books.
Burrus, V. (2007) 'Queer Father: Gregory of Nyssa and the Subversion of Identity', in Loughlin, G. (Ed.) *Queer Theology: Rethinking the Western Body*, pp. 147–162. London: Blackwell.

Carrette, J. (2001) Radical Heterodoxy and the Indecent Proposal of Erotic Theology: Critical Groundwork for Sexual Theologies. *Literature and Theology* 15(3), pp. 286–298.

Cervantes Ortiz, L. (2016) '"Lifting up God's Skirt": The Postmodern, Post-liberationist and Postcolonial Theology of Marcella Althaus-Reid: A Latin American Approach', in Panotto, N. (Ed.) *Indecent Theologies: Marcella Althaus-Reid and the Next Generation of Postcolonial Activists*, pp. 25–40. California: Borderless Press.

Cheng, P. S. (2011) *Radical Love: An Introduction to Queer Theology*. New York: Seabury Books.

Cherry, K. (2007) *Art That Dares. Gay Jesus, Woman Christ and More*. California: AndroGyne Press.

Córdova Quero, M. H. (2004) 'Friendship with Benefits: A Queer Reading of Aelred of Rievaulx and His Theology of Friendship', in Althaus-Reid, M. and Isherwood, L. (Eds.) (2004), *The Sexual Theologian*, pp. 26–46. London: Continuum.

Córdova Quero, M. H. (2006) 'The Prostitutes Also Go into the Kingdom of God: A Queer Reading of Mary of Magdala', in Althaus-Reid, M. (Ed.) *Liberation Theology and Sexuality (Second Edition)*, pp. 81–110. London: SCM Press.

Cornwall, S. (2011) *Controversies in Queer Theology*. London: SCM Press.

Cornwall, S. (2017) *Un/familiar Theology. Reconceiving Sex, Reproduction and Generativity*. London: Bloomsbury.

Garrigan, S. (2009) Queer Worship. *Theology & Sexuality*, 15(2), pp. 211–230.

Glaser, C. (1998) *Coming Out As Sacrament*. Louisville, KY: Westminster John Knox Press.

Goss, R. E. (1993) *Jesus Acted Up. A Gay and Lesbian Manifesto*. San Francisco: Harper.

Goss, R. E. (2000) 'Passionate Love for Christ: Out of the Closet, Into the Streets', in Kay, K., Nagle, J. and Gould, B. (Eds.) *Male Lust: Pleasure, Power and Transformation*, pp. 297–304. New York: Harrington Park Press.

Greenough, C. (2018) *Undoing Theology: Life Stories from Non-normative Christians*. London: SCM Press.

Guest, D. (2008) 'Liturgy and Loss: A Lesbian Perspective on using Psalms of Lament in Liturgy', in Burns, S., Jagessar, M. N. and Slee, N. (Eds.) *The Edge of God: New Liturgical Texts and Contexts in Conversation*, pp. 202–216. London: Epworth Press.

Hinkle, C. (2007) 'Love's Urgent Longings: St John of the Cross', in Loughlin, G. (Ed.) *Queer Theology: Rethinking the Western Body*, pp. 188–199. London: Blackwell.

Hollywood, A. (2007) 'Queering the Beguines: Mechthild of Magdeburg, Hadewijch of Anvers, Marguerite Porete', in Loughlin, G. (Ed.) *Queer Theology: Rethinking the Western Body*, pp. 163–175. London: Blackwell.

Isherwood, L. and Althaus-Reid, M. (2004) 'Queering Theology', in Althaus-Reid, M. and Isherwood, L. (Eds.) *The Sexual Theologian*, pp. 1–15. London: Continuum.

Larrimore, M. (2015) 'Introduction', in Talvacchia, K. T., Pettinger, M. F. and Larrimore, M. (Eds.) *Queer Christianities. Lived Religion in Transgressive Forms*, pp. 1–10. New York: New York University Press.

Loughlin, G. (2007) 'Introduction: The End of Sex', in Loughlin, G. (Ed.) *Queer Theology: Rethinking the Western Body*, pp. 1–34. London: Blackwell.

Loughlin, G. (2008) What is Queer? Theology after Identity. *Theology & Sexuality*, 14(2), pp. 143–152.

Stringer, M. (2000) Of Gin and Lace: Sexuality, Liturgy and Identity among Anglo-Catholics in the Mid-Twentieth Century. *Theology & Sexuality*, 13, pp. 35–54.

Stuart, E. (Ed.) (1997) *Religion is a Queer Thing*. London: Cassell.

Stuart, E. (2003) *Gay and Lesbian Theologies: Repetitions and Critical Difference*. Hampshire: Ashgate.

Stuart, E. (2007) 'Sacramental Flesh', in Loughlin, G. (Ed.) *Queer Theology: Rethinking the Western Body*, pp. 65–75. London: Blackwell.

Stuart, E. (2010) 'Making No Sense: Liturgy as Queer Space', in Isherwood, L. and Petrella, I. (Eds.) *Dancing Theology in Fetish Boots: Essays in Honour of Marcella Althaus-Reid*, pp. 113–123. London: SCM Press.

Tonstad, L. (2018) *Queer Theology. Beyond Apologetics*. Eugene: Wipf and Stock.

3

QUEER THEOLOGIES IN GLOBAL CONTEXTS

This chapter draws attention to the social backdrops and global contexts in which queer theologies are produced. First, attention turns to the relationship between queer theory and postcolonial criticism. Throughout the discussion the idea of fusion and encounters between cultures is prominent. The chapter then offers brief overviews of queer theologies emerging in global contexts, including Asian American, Asian, African, Latin American, Black and womanist queer theologies, as well as in the North Atlantic (Canada, UK, and USA) and Australia. While the overviews in each section provide examples of the queer theologies in situated contexts, they are by no means comprehensive. The content of each chapter should be read in conjunction with other sections of the book, where the scholarship is international in scope.

POSTCOLONIAL AND QUEER CRITICISMS

Throughout history, different countries have exercised their control over others. Colonialism refers to the political control of one country by another, by populating it with migrants and exploiting inhabitants in terms of labour. Postcolonialism examines the impact this has had. It uncovers the lasting effects of colonialism in former colonies. Stemming from this, postcolonial theology examines the impact of colonialism in relation to Christianity, particularly as aspects of the tradition have also engaged in colonisation through those who promoted Christianity in foreign lands, known as missionaries. The version of Christianity they brought was based on western contexts and values, rather than local contexts, values, and practices.

Hong Kong-born feminist theologian Kwok Pui-lan offers a reading of postcolonial theologies from a feminist perspective in her book *Postcolonial Imagination and Feminist Theology* (Kwok, 2005), where she examines the relationship between postcolonialism and issues of sexuality and gender. She states how theology is 'almost a generation behind postcolonial studies in other fields' (2005: 149). One of her aims in this project is to 'write back to a masculinist theological tradition defined by white, middle-class, Eurocentric norms' (2005: 144). She sees this as a task which welcomes wider participation from those who are feminist or pro-feminist and are committed to working with a postcolonial lens. Kwok states how reading theology with a postcolonial lens requires theologians to think in new ways. The task is one of 'redoing theology' (2005: 144). In a reading of queer theologies, Kwok is saddened that the existing scholarship 'gives the erroneous impression that the struggles of gay, lesbian, bisexual and transgendered people are transhistorical and everywhere the same' (2005: 142). The point of contextual theology is to show how beliefs about God and the practices of those beliefs are not the same everywhere, nor have they always been the same throughout history.

Kwok sees the work of writers such as Robert Goss's *Jesus Acted Up* (1993) and Elizabeth Stuart's *Religion is a Queer Thing* (1997) as 'white queer theology' (Kwok, 2005: 141). She goes further back in the lineage of queer theory, noting how both Michel Foucault and Judith Butler did not take race or colonialism into account in their work. From its inception, queer theory has been considered to be white and western. In fact the idea that queer theologies have been a largely western practice is highlighted in the subtitle of Loughlin's volume, 'Rethinking the Western Body' (Loughlin, 2007). Cornwall notes how there are differences and tensions between queer and postcolonial theologies. She cautions wisely that queer may 'be responsible for reinscribing a normativity of its own' (Cornwall, 2016: 15), where that normativity is thought of as white and western.

Can queer and postcolonial critiques come together? Intercontinental philosophy, postmodern thought, and contextualisation are used as platforms for both queer and postcolonial critiques. Jeremy Punt looks specifically at the intersections of queer theory and postcolonial theory (Punt, 2008). He is careful to warn how, 'to be clear, the theoretical and other conflicts between them should not be diminished, or the complex and conflicted, the diverse and hybrid natures of Postcolonial and Queer theories denied' (2008: 24.2). Punt makes a number of observations in the work of both frameworks. First, he notes the similarities between queer and postcolonial thought: 'Queer theory's link with post-modern and postcolonial thought already emerges when it engages the social order from the underside of the society, and necessarily questions patterns which are presented as conventional, normal, traditional, or established' (2008: 24.3). Second, both queer and postcolonial theories place strong emphasis on identity and social locations, including the notion of hybrid or multiple identities. Punt notes, 'Queer and Postcolonial theories entertain what, in biblical studies discourse, can be called a prophetic vision for the world, recognising the stakes involved in common struggles as well in the specificity and partiality of respective histories and reali-ties'(2008: 24.7). Third, Punt observes how postcolonial and queer theories intersect in the questioning of universal or dominant norms. He states, 'Like Postcolonial theory, Queer theory theorises human existence, life and society in ways necessarily different to the contemporary, conventional societal patterns' (2008: 24.6).

In her work on postcolonial criticism, Sharon Bong describes Christianity in Asia as part of 'its colonial heritage and its burden', and that the Bible is 'the colonial text' (Bong, 2006: 497). Bong discusses how the word 'post-colonial' is problematic, as it derives from 'colonialism', so the word 'post-colonial' becomes sub-ordinate to the category 'colonialism'. Postcolonialism 'ironically reinstates the structures of domination that it purports to avoid' (2006: 511). Following Sara Ahmed, Bong highlights a further problem with the term 'post-colonialism' as it implies that 'colo-nialism has been overcome in the present' (Bong, 2006: 498; Ahmed, 2000: 10). Bong emphasises the importance of exploring the needs of particularised contexts, as this 'serves as a touchstone in authenticating theologizing by, of and for Asians' (Bong, 2006: 511). She states that 'theologizing in a "post-colonial" context … involves strange encounters' (2006: 498).

In a similar vein, Rasiah Sugirtharajah (2004) draws on the idea of a blending of cultures in his work on postcolonial theology in India. He notices the reluctance of systematic theology to address the relationship between colonialism and the field of study. Sugirtharajah exposes how there was a reluctance in parts of India to criticise colonialism, as the Christian missionaries offered welfare to many people disadvantaged due to the caste system. He notes how many early converts sought to present themselves as patriotic Indians, claiming how Christianity was not a strange religion but a part of the Vedic tradition. In doing this, Sugirtharajah states how 'they raided their own textual archives to demonstrate that these Vedic texts were already Christian or modernist, so that conversion to Christianity was not in any way an act of disloyalty to India' (Sugirtharajah, 2004: 31). Christian theologies in India were formed in response to colonialism, but also as an act of nation building. Sugirtharajah discusses how theologies in India 'are mainly about belonging and identity and how Indian Christians have negotiated and continue to negotiate an Indian-Christian identity' (2004: 35). He notes how 'it appears that a theological imagination need not be in harmony with a specific geographic terrain' (2004: 36). One option is 'to blend creatively cosmopolitan and vernacular cultures' (2004: 37). He advocates that this does not involve blending into someone else's culture, which leads to a loss of identity and history, but 'the blending into one's own culture some of the liberative elements of someone else's' (2004: 37–38).

Bong and Sugirtharajah are not alone in drawing on the idea of encounters, fusion, and interaction. Gloria Anzaldúa draws attention to this in her work *Borderlands/La Frontera: The New Mestiza* (Anzaldúa, 1987). In drawing on her identities as lesbian and *chicana* (a woman of Mexican origin), Anzaldúa exposes the idea of invisible 'borders' that exist between various groups of people: Latinas/os–non-Latinas/os, men–women, heterosexuals–homosexuals, and other groups. The *mestiza* is a term used to describe a woman of indigenous and Hispanic descent in Latin America. This *mestiza* follows the idea of a 'mix', according to Anzaldúa, where cultural and spiritual values are transferred from one culture to another.

Marcella Althaus-Reid observes how postcolonial theologies and liberation theologies then risk becoming a 'theme park' of theology (Althaus-Reid, 2000). She reveals how postcolonial theologies can be seen by some in the west as novelties or area categories. She says 'people in the West are encouraged to visit them as if going to a botanical garden' (2000: 42), warning that they may seem to be regarded as an excursion. According to Althaus-Reid, 'the fact of being presented as a theme park accentuates the imaginary aspect of the construction of regional theologies. They highlight by their mere native presence the fact that real theologies are elsewhere' (2000: 42). This is one area in which queer and postcolonial theologies are a catalyst for disruption to the systematic theology of the west. Althaus-Reid continues, 'the point is precisely one of opening borders and tunnels under the theoretical construction of the West' (2000: 45). In turn, queer and postcolonial theologies are able to challenge the dominant and hegemonic nature of systematic theology within the discipline.

In some sense, queer and postcolonial theologies are a form of practical theology, engaging with individuals and communities in order to formulate theologies. What follows is a brief overview of the themes and concerns that emerge when examining queer theologies in global contexts: Asian American queer theologies, Asian queer theologies, African queer theologies, Latin American queer theologies, Black and womanist queer theologies, and queer theologies from Canada, the UK, USA, and Australia. In this overview, rather than presenting a 'theme park' description, I focus on how these theologies work to disrupt traditional theology and work on a practical level in their various contexts. Moreover, one of the limitations in this discussion is that the texts cited are written in English. I am aware of the limitations of my scope in being unable to access texts which may be written in the native languages of these locations. I am also conscious that my aim is not to offer a ventriloquist voice when discussing queer theologies in global contexts. To avoid this pitfall I have drawn heavily on global scholarship in queer theologies, and I encourage readers to explore these texts for themselves. Moreover, there is a risk that the global locations described below are interpreted as monolithic. I agree with Mary Ann Tolbert who states that there is 'no one feminist perspective or feminist reading of a text … no one womanist perspective, no one Hispanic perspective, no one Asian perspective, no one lesbian perspective, and so on' (Tolbert, 1995: 273). Tolbert is not attempting to deny the importance of social location and identity, rather she cautions how these experiences should not be thought of as universal to each particular context. The reading of the different queer theologies in global contexts in this chapter follows this principle:

that social locations, identities, and contexts allow for a range of plural experiences, identities, and voices. Moreover, queer ruptures categories of essentialism, so queer readings should not be thought of as universal or homogenised in any way.

ASIAN AMERICAN QUEER THEOLOGIES

Patrick Cheng is a leading researcher of Asian American queer theologies. His work 'marks and celebrates an emerging theological and religious scholarship among people of Asian descent who self-identify as "queer" – that is, lesbian, gay, bisexual, transgender, intersex, queer, questioning, and two-spirited folk, as well as our allies' (Cheng, 2011: 236). Using the metaphor of the rainbow, he explores the themes of multiplicity, diaspora, and hybridity in examining the experiences of queer Asian North American people of faith and suggests what queer Asian theologies may look like. In his examination of multiplicity, Cheng explores the coexistence of multiple identities – Asian, queer, spiritual, religious. He notes how even within each of these markers of identity there are further multiple identities. The idea of diaspora features prominently in his work, as it describes the reality of the experiences of many Asian North Americans who never feel quite at home. Cheng says 'we constantly experience the annoying questions of "where are you *really* from?" or "where are you *originally* from?"' (2011: 244). The idea of diaspora also extends to the fact that within the corpus of LGBTQ+ literature on religion and spirituality 'there has been virtually no reflection on the experiences of queer Asian people in those works' and that they 'are almost uniformly silent on the queer Asian experience' (2011: 245). The sense of hybridity in queer Asian North American identities relates to similar ideas noted above from Bong, Sugirtharajah, and Anzaldúa from their different geographical locations. Cheng states how 'queer Asians of faith live and exist in a "third space" that is created by the intersections of our sexualities on the one hand, and our racial identities on the other' (2011: 246).

For Cheng, marginalisation and oppression are intersectional, and he refers to the experience of discrimination through belonging to multiple minority groups. His reading of queer is in relation to sexual identities, rather than engaging with the theory of queer being anti-identity. In describing his own self-identification, Cheng is a 'rainbow theologian. Not a liberation theologian, not a post-colonial theologian, and not a queer theologian, although I do draw upon – and am indebted to elements of – each of those traditions' (Cheng, 2011: 248). For Cheng to self-identify as a rainbow theologian is to reflect the complexities of his position: multiple markers of identification, a sense of being displaced, and the occupation of a liminal, third space, where the complexities of what could be incompatible or competing identities are played out.

In outlining Asian American queer theologies, Cheng uses a method of reflecting on how the Christian tradition is multiple. He offers numerical examples by referring to four gospel writers and the Trinitarian idea of God as three in one. The experience of diaspora is described as the feeling of not being at home due to one's race and sexuality, but also due to the focus on family values in Asian communities. This exclusion becomes a double exclusion in the Church and Christian theology – 'a world that often refuses to understand how the Gospel is inextricably tied to both our sexual and racial identities' (Cheng, 2011: 251).

How the concept of hybridity informs queer Asian practices, according to Cheng, is seen in his description of how he brings Asian meditation practices into Christian worship. Cheng envisages an Asian Christology in the form of Christ as a '"third thing", between the divine and the human' (2011: 253). The idea of 'rainbow theology' is not unique to Asian people and it requires deeper engagement with queer Black, Latin American, and African American communities and contexts. This theology 'must continue to be rooted in praxis and social activism' (2011: 258). For Cheng, rainbow theology must also engage with questions of class and economic justice.

ASIAN QUEER THEOLOGIES

Joseph N. Goh is committed to exploring queer theologies from Asia. In his research, Goh describes the Malaysian *mak nyahs*, who are male-to-female transsexuals, some of whom are also sex workers. The *mak nyahs* experience discrimination and persecution because they challenge the heteronormative values of both Islamic and

Christian traditions in Malaysia. Goh's work draws parallels between how Malaysian society often attempts to regulate the bodies of the *mak nyas* in a similar way to how Christian theology has regulated the body of Mary, making her virginity sacred. With enforced regulation on their bodies, the *mak nyahs* reveal how their sexuality and gender become a vehicle that allows them to express their spirituality. Goh sees this as connected to Mary's story, as for both Mary and the *mak nyahs* 'bodily and godly experiences are inexorably intertwined, even if these experiences are sometimes fraught with ambivalent views and feelings' (Goh, 2012: 229). The bodies of Mary and the *mak nyas* are therefore both sacred. Goh also works on exploring the intersections of sexuality and faith in Malaysian gay and bisexual men (Goh, 2018).

In Hong Kong, Yip Lai-shan conducts research through interviews with non-heterosexual individuals exploring sexuality and faith, examining the experience of queer Catholics. She holds research interests in Christian sexual ethics and has published widely on these themes in Chinese. Also in Hong Kong, a recent study by Chan Pui-man (2018) examines three pro-LGBT religious groups, exploring how some organisations are working towards inclusive membership which welcomes diverse social minorities, as well as LGBTQ+ people. Chan's study details the fellowship and activities within the alliance of 'The Rainbow Covenant'. In one example from an inclusive church, pastor Susan comments:

> Happy enough, today's bread has been added with dried grapes and berries, various kinds of ingredients. It is exactly like how our God wants us to be, that is, having and embracing differences. Regardless of your sexuality, gender, race, occupation, and identity, we welcome you to our Holy Holy Communion [*sic*] (Chan, 2018: 1461).

Kwok notes how 'sexual theology has a relatively short history in Asia, and many Asian churches still find it embarrassing to discuss sexual issues in public' (Kwok, 2010: 40). She states that the task for queer Asian theologies is not only to examine the body and sexuality from the Christian tradition, but also from the cultural heritage of Asia. She cites the work of Bong (2007) as an example of a queer revisionist from Asian heritage. Bong uses the images of the lesbian mother and lesbian nun to contest the idea of womanhood, motherhood, and heterosexuality in Christianity. The queer theologies that emerge from Asia are primarily concerned with the issue of sexuality and gender through lived experiences. In many ways, queer Asian theologies engage in a project which reads religion and its impact on the lives of Christians in terms of their gender and sexuality.

Queering Migrations: Towards, From, Beyond Asia (Córdova Quero, Goh & Sepidoza Campo, 2014) examines the intersection of ethnicity, migration, sexuality, and religion. Looking towards, from, and beyond Asia, the authors engage with living experiences of LGBTQ+ people. In one example, Kunisuke Hirano tells the stories of those he calls 'sexiles', who are people who leave their country because of their sexual identifications. For the 'sexiles', migration offers promises of a better life as the expectation that people are heterosexual still holds strong in Japanese culture and society. Although the authors are less concerned with engaging with queer theologies or queer religion, the text illuminates the lives of individuals through the lens of the connection of queerness with race and ethnicity. What holds strong in this discussion is how the social and cultural presumptions of heterosexuality are inextricably linked to religion, as if heterosexuality is divine desire and any deviation from this is a crime against God. Also in Japan, Yuri Horie (2007) explores the relatively invisible existence of lesbian people in public discussions of homosexuality. She describes the mobilisation of women's activism in response to homophobic discrimination experienced by a gay man in the United Church of Christ in Japan, a Protestant church. The resistance activism was formed by women, including lesbians, bisexuals, and heterosexuals, as Horie notes that the women saw parallels between the sexism they experienced and homophobia. She situates the women's activism in this context within the thought of Adrienne Rich's 'lesbian continuum' (see Chapter 1 for more on Rich).

Within India we see how there was never legislation in place against same-sex relations until the era of British rule, when homosexuality was made a criminal offence. In 2018 the Supreme Court legalised homosexuality in India, though there is currently no recognition of same-sex unions. Despite the legal move, LGBTQ+ people still often face discrimination. George

Zachariah and Vincent Rajkumar work to bring LGBTQ+ voices into dialogue with Christian communities. Their edited book, *Disruptive Faith, Inclusive Communities: Church and Homophobia* (Zachariah & Rajkumar, 2015), presents a collection of chapters seeking to transform Christian faith communities and to promote inclusion and justice for LGBTQ+ people. In a similar vein of working with church communities in India, Philip Kuruvilla edited a volume entitled *Christian Responses to Issues of Human Sexuality and Gender Diversity: A Guide to the Churches in India* (Kuruvilla, 2017). His volume is aimed primarily at church leaders and church communities, but is also for parents, families, teachers, and friends who wish to understand more about LGBTQ+ issues and lives.

AFRICAN QUEER THEOLOGIES

Adriaan van Klinken and Lilly Phiri observe that 'Africa is now widely associated with homophobia and is even considered to be the worst continent to be gay' (van Klinken & Phiri, 2015: 36). The idea that queer theologies could emerge from such a setting seems to be at odds with the legal situations in a large number of African countries, as well as the 'traditional' views on Christianity held across the continent. At the time of writing, data from Amnesty International show how the death penalty for engaging in homosexual acts remains in force in the following African countries and regions: Mauritania, Sudan, northern Nigeria, and southern Somalia. Moreover, countries where same-sex acts or relationships are outlawed include: Algeria, Angola, Burundi, Cameroon, Comoros, Egypt, Eritrea, Ethiopia, Gambia, Ghana, Guinea, Kenya, Liberia, Libya, Malawi, Mauritania, Mauritius, Morocco, Namibia, Nigeria, Senegal, Sierra Leone, Somalia, South Sudan, Sudan, Swaziland, Tanzania, Togo, Tunisia, Uganda, Zambia, and Zimbabwe. It is legal to engage in same-sex activities and relationships within the remaining countries: Benin, Botswana, Burkina Faso, Cape Verde, Central African Republic, Chad, Congo-Brazzaville, Ivory Coast, Democratic Republic of Congo, Djibouti, Equatorial Guinea, Gabon, Guinea-Bissau, Lesotho, Madagascar, Mali, Mozambique, Niger, Rwanda, São Tomé and Principe, Seychelles, and South Africa.[1]

During the 19th century Christianity was brought to many African countries. The role of missionaries was to spread Christianity and to encourage indigenous people to convert to Christianity. The missionaries brought with them very strict moral views of sex and sexuality, which were adopted by converts. Therefore, it is important to remember that discussions of sexual relationships and Christianity in Africa are often based on the conservative British Victorian attitudes of the missionaries. These attitudes have taken hold and have been repeated socially and culturally. To a large extent these conservative values have been adopted and are now entwined with African values. These values create ideas of 'decency' which are firmly held, and thereby exclude non-heterosexual activities as not Christian and, therefore, not African. This seems somewhat ironic as it transpires that, in precolonial times, attitudes to same-sex relationships were less hostile than they appear to be today. Van Klinken and Ezra Chitando observe the following:

> indigenous African societies and cultures were characterised by a relative culture of discretion, allowing a certain space for ambiguous gender identities and non-heterosexual practices, which was then restricted by the imposition of strict gender and sexual norms by missionaries and colonial administrators (van Klinken & Chitando, 2016: 4).

Where Christian values have become intertwined with cultural and social attitudes towards same-sex relationships, it seems that there is a common perception that homosexuality is an import from western society and is therefore un-African. Moreover, these traditional values are often debated and contested on the world stage, as African Christianity plays a major role in the global Anglican Communion. In this context, religious leaders from African countries have often publicly opposed progressive stances regarding LGBTQ+ acceptance within church communities.

One of the first texts tackling the subject of same-sex desire, relationships, and Christianity in South Africa was *Aliens in the Household of God: Homosexuality and Christian Faith in South Africa* (Germond & De Gruchy, 1997). The book explores the challenges, prejudices, and discrimination experienced by gay people in South Africa, noting that the problem is not homosexuality but heterosexism. The book contains various accounts and testimonies from people's lives and their relationships with the church and community in South Africa.

In working with African church leaders and theological educators, Gerald West, Charlene van der Walt, and Kapya John Kaoma note the new site of struggle for Christianity in Africa is the presence of LGBTQ+ people and homophobia (West, van der Walt & Kapya, 2016). They state how the lived realities of LGBTQ+ experiences are important to inform theologies on sexualities. They call for a process of 'people's theology':

> people's theology is not simply a step on the way to the 'real' thing; people's theology is the real thing. It is the theology of the people in that it seeks to address the contradiction between the visible people and the invisible people. People's theology does not rest on definitions that reject 'other people' in favour of 'the people', but seeks to acknowledge the sacredness of all human beings, even those who are rendered invisible, as the image of the Creator (West, van der Walt & Kapya, 2016: 2).

This is a theology that does not focus on the centre of power in theology, as traditional theology and the Bible 'have usually been whips to chastise' LGBTQ+ people (West, van der Walt & Kapya, 2016: 2), and focusing on the centre 'is to participate in the violence perpetrated by the centre' (2016: 3). The authors call for queer Christians to reclaim their presence in theology: 'queer Christians must be thoroughly theologically equipped to re-encounter the very tradition that has tormented and traumatised them' (2016: 3).

Van Klinken has become a prominent and eminent scholar on the issue of non-normative sexuality and emerging queer theologies in Africa, and his exceptional work deserves closer examination in this section. His 2013 book, *Transforming Masculinities in African Christianity: Gender Controversies in Times of AIDS,* explores African Christian theological discussions around the ideas of gender, specifically masculinity in light of the HIV/AIDS epidemic. Van Klinken's work forms part of 'the emerging (but contested) body of queer studies in Africa' (van Klinken 2015: 948).

The reason queer studies have been contested as a possible site of inquiry within Africa is due to their history and perception as white, western thought. Van Klinken discusses the '(im)possibility of African queer studies' (van Klinken, 2017: np), referring to scholars who consider queer studies a western project and who question whether the approaches could work in African contexts at all. He states, 'queer studies, if it really takes seriously African queer subjectivity, must contend with the fact that many LGBT people in Africa identify with the same religious traditions that are so vocal against them' (2017: np). He warns that non-African scholars working on African queer theologies should be sensitive to local politics, ways of naming, and theorising by working from grass-roots culture.

Van Klinken and Phiri's work explores the development of queer theologies in African contexts. Like many queer theologies emerging in global contexts, for van Klinken and Phiri the queer project must begin with real lives of marginalised sexualities, so they focus on gay men in Zambia for their study. They point to the importance of grounding theology about non-normative sexualities in marginalised, contested settings:

> queer theology puts sexuality in all its varieties central in the understanding of the image of God. This is certainly relevant in African contexts where certain forms of sexuality have recently become heavily policed and politicized, and where same-sex loving people have been excluded and marginalized (van Klinken and Phiri, 2015: 44).

Within the Zambian context of the study, participants believe that discrimination against homosexuality is a result of dominant Pentecostal Christian beliefs and that homosexuals are viewed as 'the Devil or the Antichrist' (van Klinken and Phiri, 2015: 45). Gay participants in the study believe God created them as children of God and that 'God is indifferent to sexuality' (2015: 47). Van Klinken and Phiri acknowledge that a grassroots study of gay Christian men does not set the standard for African queer theologies, and they state how other people from the LGBTQ+ community need to have their voices heard. An African grassroots theology allows people to think about being made in the image of God in contextual queer ways. Again, though, we are warned to pay particular attention to context in formulating queer theologies, as 'queer theology in Africa is possible and timely – but only if it takes cognizance of the social, cultural and political specificities and sensitivities in African contexts' (2015: 45). This question of specificities and sensitivities must extend to the labelling of Africa as a homophobic continent. Ryan Thoreson (2014) is keen to point out that local understandings of same-sex attitudes can differ and that homophobia is difficult to define, as is being able to identify possible 'rises' or 'falls' in homophobia in Africa. Thoreson states that to describe Africa as a homophobic continent would be racist as it would 'leave little room for the nuance and specificity of sexual politics' (Thoreson, 2014: 24).

Despite the fact that religion is often cited as being a source for homophobia in African contexts, van Klinken notes how religion is also a source for self-affirmation: 'while religion is generally considered a key factor contributing to homophobia in contemporary Africa, it also appears to be a resource for queer subjectivity and empowerment' (van Klinken, 2015: 960). Further examples of empowerment from grassroots contexts are found in the daily lives and experiences of queer Africans. Embracing the use of digital technologies where available, the voices of African queer women have been heard through an online project, Hub of Loving Action in Africa (HOLAA!).[2] While not necessarily engaging directly with the question of religion as part of religious experience, HOLAA! does allow for discussions on sex, sexuality, and the African experience within public forums. Furthermore, stories of African queer lives are also found in emerging literature, such as *Stories of Our Lives* (The Nest Collective, 2015), where several of the narratives engage with the topic of Christianity.

In a commitment to mobilising living experience as a source for theology, van Klinken uses autobiography as a source for African queer theologies (van Klinken, 2018). In adhering to prioritising context, van Klinken develops grassroots queer theologies in which individuals recall their own queer experiences and identities, countering claims that queer is 'un-African' and 'un-Christian'. He states how 'Queer stories remain generally untold and queer voices remain largely muted in African theology' (2018: 128). The turn to life story research demonstrates how African queer theologies are not a theoretical task: 'African queer theology is not to be developed "out of the blue" but is already present in the stories of African

LGBTI people of faith' (2018: 213). Van Klinken states how 'African theology should be written in such a way that African queer people can locate themselves within it, and that queer life stories are the starting point for this' (2018: 217). The task to locate and tell these stories is one which is beginning to take shape. As van Klinken states, 'queer storytelling is key to the development of grassroots African queer theologies and to disrupting the silence and taboo surrounding sexual diversity in hegemonic African Christianities and theologies' (2018: 229). The importance of sharing stories as a wider strategy for queer theologies is discussed further in Chapter 5.

LATIN AMERICAN QUEER THEOLOGIES

Born in Rosario, Argentina, Marcella Althaus-Reid was a Latin American theologian whose work had a profound effect on the areas of liberation, feminist, and queer theologies. The influence of her living experiences in Latin American contexts is detailed throughout her scholarship (Chapter 2 details her work on *Indecent Theology*). In grounding her theologies in real lives she describes her style of theology as a *caminata* – a walk with others. She states how 'this theological journey involves taking risks' (Althaus-Reid, 2004: 2), as queer theologians embark on 'a path from the margins of sexual and economic exclusion' (2004: 4). The path explores two issues which have been taboo in Christian theology: sexuality and poverty. This is one of the main reasons why liberation theology and, subsequently, queer theologies have engaged with the issue of economy and capitalism.

Gabriela González Ortuño describes Althaus-Reid's theology as shockingly refreshing, 'a bucket of cold water' (González Ortuño, 2016: 94). By basing her theology in the lives of everyday marginalised people in Latin America – such as the poor lemon vendors, the frequenters of gay bars who carry rosaries, or the fetishists – Althaus-Reid searches for theological explanations that 'bring us closer to the idea of a queer God; that is, a God which does not reflect the dominant male in the work of most theologians' (2016: 90). For Althaus-Reid then, there is a need for sexual honesty in theology:

> Queer theology is a process of Outing Theology as a method for action and reflection, in the sense that, first of all, Classical theology needs to come clean with its real sexual identity, from where goals and objectives can be worked out. I have said elsewhere, that all theology is sexual theology, it is just that traditionally theology doesn't admit it. It is still in the closet about its true sexual nature (Althaus-Reid, 2001: 60).

Althaus-Reid's innovations, insights, and passions are further revealed by the authors of the essays edited by Nicolas Panotto, *Indecent Theologians: Marcella Althaus-Reid and the Next Generation of Postcolonial Activism* (Panotto, 2016). Some of the essays and contributions are grounded in Latin American contexts and many essays were translated from the original languages in which they were written. These essays demonstrate that there is much more indecent theologising to do. In one example, reflecting on the real lives of the poorest people in Brazil, Claudio Carvalhaes echoes Althaus-Reid's previous claims that liberation theology has shied away from talking about 'the body and the sexual themes in the life of the poor: desire, sexual drives, unfitted sexual behaviors, sexualized notions of the subject, sexual (dis)orientations, transgressions' (Carvalhaes, 2016: 157). Carvalhaes cites the problems of patriarchy, racism, and homophobia as reasons why such themes have been ignored. More importantly, he reveals how the history of postcolonialism has had a major impact on the self-understanding of Latin American people: 'the represented *self*, constructed and imposed by the *conquistador* over the colonized bodies and minds of Latin American people, has still affected the ways in which we see ourselves' (2016: 206).

The idea of listening to life stories and experiences of queer people is a feature of the work by James B. Nickoloff. He cites relationality, homosexuality, community, and family as important features in US Latino/a theology. Nickoloff states that the effect of listening to the voices of the sexually marginalised does more for the wider community than it does for the individuals telling their story. He states, 'it would make the community more genuinely "Hispanic" – that is, more truly mestiza, more deeply interconnected, and more authentically loving' (Nickoloff, 2003: 32).

In working with families and communities, Miguel De La Torre authored a bilingual book entitled *A La Familia: A Conversation about Our Families, the Bible, Sexual Orientation and Gender* (De La Torre, 2011). The book seeks to promote the inclusion of LGBTQ+ people in Latin American communities. The text was created by Latin American communities for their communities. It has three main aims: to offer advice on approaching healthy conversations among Latin American families with regards to sexual orientation, gender identity, and religion; to build Latin American communities; and to encourage Latin American leaders of faith to strive for full inclusion.

In *The Wiley Blackwell Companion to Latino/a Theology* (2015), Robyn Henderson-Espinoza's essay tackles Latin American theology from a queer perspective. In the essay, 'Queer Theory and Latina/o Theologizing' (Henderson-Espinoza, 2015), three major characteristics of Latin American theology are highlighted: *cotidiano* (everyday), *conjunto* (togetherness), and movement. *Cotidiano* relates to everyday life, while *conjunto* is something done together, in community. Henderson-Espinoza discusses how narrative has been used as an organising feature in Latin American theology in order to tell a story. Using the gender-neutral adjective Latin@, Henderson-Espinoza explains how Latin@ queer theologies use storytelling to draw attention to the role of sexuality, desire, and identity. Building on the idea of a *mestiza*, Henderson-Espinoza adapts this idea from Latin American queer theorist Gloria Anzaldúa, who uses the term to describe how mixedness and in-betweenness are characteristic of queerness. Henderson-Espinoza notes how the idea of being mixed or in-between becomes a useful methodology as it allows for intersections of theory, race, ethnicity, and theology. In one example, the idea of the family is developed as a *mestiza*, as queer people may need to choose between biological family or the family developed through friendships, and this in itself queers the idea of the traditional family.

BLACK AND WOMANIST QUEER THEOLOGIES

Black is often written with a capital B to refer to people from African heritage, black with a small b is simply a colour: this is a custom I adopt here as the majority of authors I engage with follow this practice. Moreover, a similar practice does not exist with 'white' so there is no reason to capitalise. Black and womanist theologies emerged in the USA, confronting questions of race and ethnicity. Black theology emerged as a liberation theology. In brief, Black theology is concerned with the experience of being Black in the world as well as economic deprivation, given that Black history is so heavily punctuated with the history of slavery. In 1969 James Cone authored *Black Theology and Black Power*. For Cone, Black theology begins with the experience of African Americans in their churches. Against a backdrop of the civil rights and Black Power movements in the USA, Cone describes Black experience as 'being Black in America has little to do with skin color. Being Black means that your heart, your soul, your mind, and your body are where the dispossessed are' (Cone, 1969: 151). Later, however, Cone examines the theme of race a little more closely. In an essay entitled 'White Theology Revisited', he criticised the white church for failing to adequately address issues of race. Black theology is rooted in Black culture, so sources from African American culture form part of the theology, including writings, music, and spirituals. A spiritual is a Christian song which describes the hard and difficult oppressions experienced under slavery. The spirituals encompass aspects of identity, faith, and the tribulations of Black people, describing the emotion and physical burden of slavery. Some spirituals, known as jubilees, look hopefully to a future of freedom.

Dolores Williams described the work of Cone as sexist, stating how he failed to account for the experiences of Black women. In 1993 she re-envisioned Black theology from a feminist perspective. As feminist theology related to the experience of white women, and Black theology was concerned with the experience of Black men, Williams became a significant figure in the development of womanist theology. The term womanist is used to describe the feminist writings about Black women and their experiences. Her text, *Sisters in the Wilderness: The Challenge of Womanist God Talk* (Williams, 1993), focuses on:

> Black women's experience to provide the lens through which we view sources, to provide the issues that form the content of our theology, and to help formulate the questions we ask about God's relation to Black American life and the world in general (Williams, 1993: 12).

Williams' text demonstrated the intersectionality of being marginalised as a woman, and then again as a Black woman. In terms of discussing sexuality, Kelly Brown Douglas's pivotal text *Sexuality and the Black Church* (Douglas, 1999) explores why the themes of sexuality are considered so taboo in Black culture. Pamela Lightsey humorously describes her delightful response on picking up Douglas's book for the first time, noting how 'we couldn't wait to get the book home, set aside our dull readings written by dead white men, and read about Black preachers having sex' (Lightsey, 2015: 4). Douglas's intention was to break the silence on Black sexuality, and she writes about the impact of HIV/AIDS on the Black community. This means that the issues can no longer be silenced. Douglas examines how the church has regulated sex, devaluing and demonising human sexuality. She says how, through the eyes of the church, sexual activity is viewed as 'passionate, irrational and even satanic behaviour' (Douglas, 1999: 29). This has enabled the church to have incredible power and control in the regulation of sexuality. In further examining the links between sexuality and power, Douglas reveals how white culture has exercised control over Black sexuality by viewing Black bodies as sensual and exotic, and for women this has resulted in vulnerability and attacks on their bodies. The colonisation of white culture on Black sexuality positions Black women as seducers and Black men as sexual predators. Douglas stands with lesbian, gay, and bisexual people by calling out homophobia as an area which also regulates sexuality within the Black community and church.

There has been a tendency in many Black communities to see homosexuality as a plague. Being gay, therefore, associates sexuality with sin. Roger Sneed's *Representations of Homosexuality* (Sneed, 2010) draws attention to the religious experiences of Black gay men. Sneed unveils how religion and theology have seen homosexuality in Black churches as a problem to be solved, therefore gay people are demonised in some way. Sneed sees the Black church as heteronormative, and, even in those where the congregations claim to be accepting, 'Black liberation theology had not progressed much beyond simplistic statements such as "God loves you"' (2010: 6). His work highlights how gay theologians have not examined Black gay experiences, and how liberation and womanist theology had not engaged with the question of sexuality. Sneed states that 'Black liberation and womanist theologies have substantively little to offer Black queers other than a rhetoric of mere tolerance' (2010: 177). According to Sneed, Black theologies have failed to recognise that queer Black experiences exist. Sneed highlights the homophobia within Black communities that causes many homosexual people to lead destructive lifestyles through lack of acceptance. He discusses 'different conceptions of God and spirituality that are open rather than closed' and how Black queer theologies dare 'to call into question the presumptive goodness of God and the efficacy of the Black church in ameliorating crises in Black sexual identity' (2010: 190). In outlining the exclusion of non-heterosexual people in liberation, Black, and womanist theologies, Sneed points to the fact that all theologies move on: 'there is no theology or ethics that remains static, unchanging and unalterable' (2010: 176).

Black women tend to make up the majority of the congregants in Black churches, although leadership is still dominated by men. In one queer interpretation of Black theology, Stephen Finley accounts for the absence of Black men from churches as he discusses how they may struggle to enter into a bodily relationship with Jesus. Finley sees 'a conflict between a masculine Black-body construct and a same-sex symbolic relationship with an all-powerful male Divinity' (Finley, 2007: 305). In his queer reading of heterosexuality, Finley engages in fieldwork research with men in a Baptist church in the USA. Using sexual metaphors, he states how some religious heterosexual Black men were unable to submit to a male God through worship, as this 'places the male in the "feminine" or passive recipient position of the relationship' (2007: 317).

What do Black queer theologies look like? E. L. Kornegay argues that 'we must accept that Black (race) is already queer. Blackness and Black theological discourse has yet to accept its own queerness' (Kornegay, 2012: 331). Race, according to Kornegay, 'rests uncomfortably in our souls' (2012: 333), and he demonstrates how queer theory exposes 'mismatches' in our identifications: gender, sex, race, religion. Such mismatches have been examined by liberational theology using a tool which stretches the imagination, and an example of this is the image of the Black Christ. Kornegay states that it is this elasticity which is used as a method which makes 'Black theology queer by definition' (2012: 334). In

2013 Kornegay wrote *A Queering of Black Theology: James Baldwin's Blues Project and Gospel Prose*, which examines writings from Baldwin, the Black novelist and social critic. Kornegay states how the book's aim is to engage in Black theology in ways that are post-civil rights, post-liberation, and postmodern. This, in turn, will enable 'faith and flourishing for the multiple representations of gendered and sexualized bodies within the black church and community' [*sic*] (2013: 1).

In offering an example of Black queer theologies which are grounded in sexual themes, Brittney Cooper sets out a Black feminist theology of pleasure. She describes how her previous writings on such matters had alienated her from her Black church communities as she received hateful responses to connecting issues of desire to Christianity. Cooper notes how 'many other Black women who read the piece called me everything but a child of God, hurled scripture like knives, and basically condemned me to hell for leading other women astray' (Cooper, 2018: 193). In highlighting how sex is somehow sinful and connected to issues of guilt and shame for Black women, Cooper says how 'they would have sex on Saturdays and put those same "sins" on the altar on Sundays' (2018: 198). Rather than see sex as something of a demon, Cooper's aim is to show it as divine. Her Black theology of pleasure releases women from experiences of guilt which is often related to sexual pleasure. Significantly, its reach goes beyond the pleasure of Black women to encompass queer lives. Black queer theologies, therefore, demand 'a forthright engagement with the politics of the Black female, queer, trans, and/or gender non-conforming body' (2018: 199).

Pamela Lightsey is a prominent figure in the writing of queer womanist theology and puts forward 'a queer womanist departure from Anglo-American queer studies' (Lightsey, 2012: 340). Rather than building her queer womanist theologies on white queer thinkers, her project is grounded in the lives and experiences of the African American community. She sees the word 'queer' as a problem, especially when used to refer to identity rather than theory. She uses humour to describe how people in the Black community respond to her when she says she is queer: '"Wha' da hell you mean 'queer'? Shiiit dat muthafucka jus' funny!"' (2012: 341). Lightsey finds use of the term 'queer' as a marker of self-identification too ambiguous and too weak. She states that, for the Black queer community, the church must come out: 'Until the Black church "comes out" and really loves its Blackness [...] it cannot love God, itself, nor its many diverse members as it ought' (2012: 347).

Lightsey also authored a text contextualising womanist queer theologies, *Our Lives Matter* (2015), the title of which adopts the slogan from the 'Black Lives Matter' campaign and national protests in the USA against police treatment of Black people. Womanist queer theologies are not only concerned with Black women, Black culture, and Black churches, as Lightsey notes:

> It would, nevertheless, be incorrect to suggest the only concern of womanist theology is Black women and Black culture. We are interested in exposing discrimination of Black women in particular and women in general. We are concerned about Black communities in particular but Creation in general. Nowadays our work is expansive addressing ecological needs, the struggle for quality education, self-care, quality of care for the poor and oppressed and so forth (Lightsey, 2015: 13).

We see how intersectional concerns become part of the project of queer theologies, reaching beyond identity-based issues but examining social-based concerns such as poverty, education, and the environment.

NORTH ATLANTIC QUEER THEOLOGIES (CANADA, UK, AND USA)

Within the North Atlantic context – the UK, USA, and Canada – queer theologies trace their lineage back to early lesbian and gay theologies (see Chapter 1 for a brief overview of lesbian and gay theologies). In highlighting the roots of this development, US theologian Robert Goss says 'the explosion of activism in the late 1980s and 1990s transformed gay theology into queer theologies and widened their dialogue partners' (Goss, 1998: 189). He draws attention to the inclusive potential of queer theologies that was lacking in gay and lesbian theologies. Goss offers one of the earliest definitions of queer relating to theology. He states:

> Queer as a verb means 'to spoil the effect of, to interfere with, to disrupt, harm, or put in a bad light'. Queering is a deconstructive critique of the homophobic and heterosexist political theology that already excludes us. It inverts cultural symbols, perverts and disrupts valued theologies and church practices that are already spoiled for us. Queering imaginatively reconstructs theology, spirituality and church practices in new, inclusive configurations (Goss, 1998: 194).

In the movement from lesbian and gay theologies to queer theologies, one area of focus is sexual theologies. In 1979 US theologian James Nelson published *Embodiment*, and the phrase 'sexual theology' began to emerge. Nelson states how 'sexual questions are also religious questions' (Nelson, 1979: 15) and advocates a move beyond looking at questions of sexual ethics within theology to examining how human sexual experience can be a grounding for theology. Nelson's thinking was courageous and ground-breaking in positioning theology from a non-traditional space that many would consider taboo. His theology looks specifically at the range of sexual practices: fantasy, masturbation, intercourse, and sado-masochism. In 1988 a further text authored by Nelson was published which specifically examined male sexuality, *The Intimate Collection (Nelson, 1988)*. Nelson's books are considered to be classic texts on sexual theology.

In the UK Adrian Thatcher presents a Christian sexual theology in his book *Liberating Sex* (1993). Thatcher states that the book is about 'a *remaking*, an *unmaking* and a *merrymaking*' (Thatcher, 1993: 1). He notes how humans, as sexual beings, are made in the image of God and 'in *remaking* us as sexual beings, God, through the Holy Spirit, gives us the power and the vision to make relationships which resemble those relationships existing eternally with God' (1993: 2). The process of *unmaking* reveals the legacy of patriarchy on the Christian tradition, while *merrymaking* 'is an antidote to the deadening seriousness that has attached itself to sexual activity in much of Christian history' (1993: 3). Thatcher engages in comprehensive discussions of human sexuality and sexual ethics based on traditional Christian theology, critical theory, and contemporary lives. The work, as a forerunner in Christian sexual theology, boldly discusses sexuality, marriage, same-sex relationships, celibacy, masturbation, and safe sex. The relationship between spirituality and sexuality, the fluidity of sexuality and gender, how the church relates to queer people, and how focusing on the erotic and embodied self can inform theology, are issues taken up by Peter Sweasey in his edited volume *From Queer to Eternity* (Sweasey, 1997). Sweasey's collection of essays spans different religions, beliefs, and spiritualities, yet he refuses to make arguments in defence of homosexuality, precisely because it needs none as it is as valid as heterosexuality.

In North Atlantic contexts we see the concerns and problems with gay and lesbian theology and the grounding of queer theologies in sexual theologies and activism. A group of Anglo-American scholars turn their attention to reading how traditional theology is already queer in *Queer Theology: Rethinking the Western Body* (Loughlin, 2007). Gerard Loughlin sees theology as queer as it is already strange and does not fit in the modern world; he observes how the call for reflection on embodiment and sexuality is one that comes from within the Christian tradition (See Chapter 2). Loughlin asserts that 'queer theology is also queer because it finds – like queer theory – that gay sexuality is not marginal to Christian thought and culture, but oddly central [...] The most orthodox turns out to be the queerest of all' (2007: 9). Loughlin observes how Christianity has always been queer, through 'the queer interests that were always at play in the Spirit's movement, in the lives and devotions of saints and sinners, theologians and ecclesiastics' (2007: 9). In the USA, Mark Jordan shares the same opinion as Loughlin, stating 'queer theology does not come after queer theory [...] it was there all along inside queer theory – and, indeed, before queer theory, as its competing parent, its disciplinary root and rival' (Jordan, 2007: 573).

UK-based scholar Susannah Cornwall has made significant contributions to the field of queer theologies, most notably in her book *Controversies in Queer Theology* (Cornwall, 2011). In a commitment to extending queer theologies beyond academic settings, Cornwall has authored church-based resources, including *Sexuality: the Inclusive Church Resource* (Cornwall, 2014). The resource is aimed at clergy and church organisations, drawing on references from the Church of England's debates on sexuality. Cornwall notes the need for church teachings and theologies to change. She states that:

> Each time and culture throws up new possibilities and new chal-
> lenges – a set of new contexts in which the Christian path must be
> outworked. The Bible does not pronounce on the use of hook-up
> apps such as Tinder and Grindr, or the ethics of internet dating. It
> does not explicitly condemn paedophilia – indeed, we might be sur-
> prised if it did, given the prevalence of sexual relationships between
> men and boys in the Greco-Roman world. It is also silent on sex toys
> and BDSM play, and muted on masturbation, oral and anal sex
> (Cornwall, 2014: 59–60).

Cornwall observes how debates on sexuality raise questions
beyond same-sex relations. Her extensive scholarship in the field
includes pioneering contributions relating specifically to intersex
and transgender theologies (see Chapter 5).

Canadian scholar Margaret Robinson has focused on bisexuality
and theology. She notes how 'traditionally, Christian theology has
ignored bisexuality, instead defining homosexuality as encompassing
all same-sex attraction and expression' (Robinson, 2015: 644).
According to Robinson, however, gay, lesbian, and queer theology
has also not given adequate space to the inclusion of bisexuality and
has actually produced scholarship which can be interpreted as 'bipho-
bic' (2015: 646). She observes three key issues in bisexual theology:

> (1) a holistic view of human sexuality [...] (2) a tendency towards synth-
> esis, unifying what are often seen as opposite categories; and (3) using an
> intersectional lens to examine how sexuality is shaped and constructed by
> categories such as class, race, or gender (Robinson, 2015: 649).

Interestingly, Robinson sees that one of the strengths of bisexual
theology is that it tends not to take up a category of its own. She
states: 'Bisexual theology's greatest contribution may be manifested
not in developing our own theological discourse – another box
labelled "bisexual theology" – but in having our theological
insights taken up by all theologians' (Robinson, 2015: 653).

AUSTRALIAN QUEER THEOLOGIES

In Australian contexts we see queer theologies in the works of Michael
Bernard Kelly and Jillian Cox. Kelly's work explores the contemporary

spirituality of gay men in two of his books, *Seduced by Grace: Contemporary Spirituality, Gay Experience and Christian Faith* (Kelly, 2007) and *Christian Mysticism's Queer Flame: Spirituality in the Lives of Contemporary Gay Men* (Kelly, 2018). Kelly's earlier work (2007) begins from his own autobiographical perspective, detailing the forced end of his career in the Catholic education service in Australia because of his homosexuality. *Seduced by Grace* is a collection of different forms of writing – letters, articles, and essays exploring the individual and personal experiences of reconciling faith and sexuality. His most recent work (2018) explores the spiritual and life journeys of eight gay men, although the participants come from the USA.

Cox's commitment to queer theologies is demonstrated in her scholarship relating to queering traditional theology, specifically focusing on the letters of Martin Luther and Paul. Although it does not focus on Australian contexts, her work is an example of scholarship that re-examines traditional theology using the lens of the queer-view mirror. In subverting what has been considered traditional or normative theology, Cox demonstrates how this can benefit queer theologies. In her reading of Luther, Cox maintains a commitment to his theology yet argues that his ethical approach is one which 'should be extended to theological response to lesbians and gays, and queer people broadly, and that the tools are present in the Lutheran tradition to achieve this' (Cox, 2013: 366). Moreover, she notes how, at the time, Luther challenged biblical and traditional theologies, and examined theologies grounded in new contexts similar to the approach of queer theologies. In her reading of Paul's letters to the Romans and Corinthians, Cox reveals how love should surpass human preoccupation with knowledge. The title of her article, 'Love is Better than Knowledge' (Cox, 2015), makes this clear. Underpinning her scholarship, Cox states: 'My argument is that a theology needs to engage scripture and tradition with secular thought to be relevant and transforming for people of faith and their communities, and that doing so will proffer better visions of what it means to be human' (2015: 54).

CONCLUSION

One emerging theme in postcolonial theologies is the notion of hybridity in relation to identity. This idea emerges in different contexts in the following examples: Cheng's idea of 'third space'

(2011), Bong's 'strange encounters' (2006), Anzaldúa's *mestiza* (1987), and Sugirtharajah's notion of 'blending' (2004). What queer and postcolonial theologies have in common is their relationship to what has been thought of as 'mainstream' or 'traditional' Christianity. Queer and postcolonial theologies expose that what we think of as mainstream or traditional theology is only considered as such because it is being performed and repeated. Queer and postcolonial theologies question and critically examine traditional Christian theology. Yet Cornwall notes how the genealogy of queer theologies may continue to be problematic for some. She states:

> Queer theology is not inherently white and Western – that is, it is not condemned to be white and Western, nor to exclude non-white cultures – but it must recognize that its genealogy in Western lesbian, gay and feminist theologies (and, most significantly, in Western Christianity) may prejudice it in this direction. It is therefore possible that there will always be people who do not feel able to place themselves under this umbrella because of uncomfortable associations with elements of its history (Cornwall, 2011: 105).

Cornwall goes on to say that postcolonial and queer theologies use a similar language in articulating their experiences and their resistance. This chapter has considered the conflicts and shared agendas of queer and postcolonial criticism, as both interrogate the theological mainstream using the tools of postmodern thought and through prioritising practical theologies grounded in living experiences in different contexts. This takes us beyond what has been established and controlled in traditional theology, as Dickinson and Toomey note:

> To queer theology, then, is to take up a posture of resistance, an attitude of questioning, and an intellect informed by deconstruction [...] A theology that is queer calls us to go beyond what is known, to move past what is established, and to relinquish control over such structures totally (Dickinson & Toomey, 2017: 13).

There is no excuse for contemporary queer theologies not to engage with intersectional approaches, as this has been voiced and repeated by feminist and queer theories that have come before. Through a commitment to intersectionality and to practical theology in global contexts, queer theologies are 'grassroots theology' suggested by van Klinken and Phiri (2015), prioritising the voices and experiences of individuals and communities. Theologising from experience requires the type of walk, *caminata*, advocated by Althaus-Reid (2004). The attention which must be given to Christian lives in the production of queer theologies is further explored in Chapter 5. For now, attention turns to queer biblical criticism.

FURTHER READING

ASIAN AMERICAN QUEER THEOLOGIES

Cheng, P. S. (2013) *Rainbow Theology: Bridging Race, Sexuality, and Spirit.* New York: Seabury Books.

Cheng provides illuminating discussion on queer and people of colour theologies, including queer Black theologies, queer Asian American theologies, and queer Latina/o theologies, as well as two-spirit indigenous scholarship.

ASIAN QUEER THEOLOGIES

http://www.queerasianspirit.org/

A website offering a basic overview of Asian queer theologies. The website offers a comprehensive list of publications for those wishing to explore more about Asian queer theologies.

AFRICAN QUEER THEOLOGIES

Van Klinken, A. and Obadare, E. (Eds.) (2019) *Christianity, Sexuality and Citizenship in Africa.* London and New York: Routledge.

This book looks at the relationship between Christianity, sexuality, and citizenship in sub-Saharan Africa, paying attention to the crisis of HIV and AIDS and the growing visibility of LGBT communities.

LATIN AMERICAN QUEER THEOLOGIES

Panotto, N. (Ed.) (2016) *Indecent Theologies: Marcella Althaus-Reid and the Next Generation of Postcolonial Activists.* California: Borderless Press.

An edited collection of essays, which focuses mainly on queer theologies in Latin America.

BLACK AND WOMANIST QUEER THEOLOGIES

Douglas, K. B. (1999) *Sexuality and the Black Church*. New York: Orbis Books.

One of the first texts exploring the importance of sexuality in the Black church. Douglas exposes how and why sexuality has been seen as taboo in Black culture, and what the churches should do to engage with issues of sexuality.

Lightsey, P. R. (2015) *Our Lives Matter: A Womanist Queer Theology*. Oregon: Pickwick Publications.

Lightsey offers an overview of the issues of sexuality and race in Black churches, as well as an introduction to queer theology from a womanist perspective. This text is clearly written.

NOTES

1 https://www.amnesty.org.uk/lgbti-lgbt-gay-human-rights-law-africa-ugan da-kenya-nigeria-cameroon
2 Hub of Loving Action in Africa (HOLAA!): http://holaafrica.org/about-us/

REFERENCES

Ahmed, S. (2000) *Strange Encounters: Embodied Others in Post-Coloniality*. London: Routledge.

Althaus-Reid, M. (2000) 'Gustavo Gutiérrez Goes to Disneyland: Theme Park Theologies and the Diaspora of the Discourse of the Popular Theologian in Liberation Theology', in Segovia, F. F. (Ed.) *Interpreting Beyond Borders*, pp. 36–58. Sheffield: Sheffield Academic Press.

Althaus-Reid, M. (2001) Outing Theology: Thinking Christianity out of the Church Closet. *Feminist Theology*, 9(27), pp. 57–67.

Althaus-Reid, M. (2004) *From Feminist to Indecent Theology*. London: SCM Press.

Anzaldúa, G. E. (1987) *Borderlands/La Frontera: The New Mestiza*. San Francisco: Aunt Lute.

Bong, S. (2006) 'Post-colonialism', in Sawyer, J. F. A. (Ed.) *The Blackwell Companion to the Bible and Culture*, pp. 497–514. Oxford: Blackwell.

Bong, S. A. (2007) 'Queer Revisions of Christianity', in Brazal, A. M. and Si, A. L. (Eds.) *Body and Sexuality: Theological-Pastoral Perspectives of Women in Asia*, pp. 234–249. Quezon City: Ateneo de Manila University Press.

Carvalhaes, C. (2016) 'Oppressed Bodies Don't Have Sex: The Blind Spots of Bodily and Sexual Discourses in the Construction of Subjectivity in Latin American Liberation Theology', in Panotto, N. (Ed.) *Indecent Theologies: Marcella Althaus-Reid and the Next Generation of Postcolonial Activists*, pp. 155–212. California: Borderless Press.

Chan, P-M. (2018) Desexualizing Sexual Identity Politics: The Framing of Pro-LGBT Christian Organizations in Hong Kong. *Sexuality & Culture*, 22 (4), pp. 1452–1465.

Cheng, P. S. (2011) The Rainbow Connection. *Theology & Sexuality*, 17(3), pp. 235–264.

Cone, J. (1969) *Black Theology and Black Power*. New York: The Seabury Press.

Cooper, B. (2018) How Sarah Got Her Groove Back, or Notes Toward a Black Feminist Theology of Pleasure. *Black Theology*, 16(3), pp. 195–206.

Córdova Quero, H., Goh, J. N. and Sepidoza Campo, M. (Eds.) (2014) *Queering Migrations: Towards, From, Beyond Asia*. New York: Palgrave Macmillan.

Cornwall, S. (2011) *Controversies in Queer Theology*. London: SCM Press.

Cornwall, S. (2014) 'A Theology of Sexuality', in Cornwall, S. (Ed.) *Sexuality: the inclusive church resource*, pp. 53–112. London: Darton, Longman and Todd.

Cornwall, S. (2016) 'Strange Encounters: Postcolonial and Queer Intersections', in Panotto, N. (Ed.) *Indecent Theologies: Marcella Althaus-Reid and the Next Generation of Postcolonial Activists*, pp. 3–24. California: Borderless Press.

Cox, J. E. (2013) 'The Only Safe Guide is Love': Models of Engaging Luther's Ethical Hermeneutic for Theological Responses to the Affirmation of Same-Sex Sexuality. *Dialog: A Journal of Theology*, 52(4), pp. 365–372.

Cox, J. E. (2015) Love is Better than Knowledge: Paul, Luther and a Theology of Being Human. *Theology & Sexuality*, 21(1), pp. 53–69.

De La Torre, M. (2011) *A La Familia: A Conversation about Our Families, the Bible, Sexual Orientation and Gender*. Available at: https://assets2.hrc.org/files/assets/resources/A_La_Familia_Final_Curriculum_Nov_2011.pdf?_ga=2.233047390.1165034153.1558376633-1850997694.1558376633

Dickinson, C. and Toomey, M. (2017) The continuing relevance of 'queer' theology for the rest of the field. *Theology & Sexuality*, 23(1–2), pp. 1–16.

Douglas, K. B. (1999) *Sexuality and the Black Church*. New York: Orbis Books.

Finley, S. (2007) Homoeroticism and the African-American Heterosexual Male: Quest for Meaning in the Black Church. *Black Theology*, 5(3), pp. 305–326.

Germond, P. and De Gruchy, S. (Eds.) (1997) *Aliens in the Household of God: Homosexuality and Christian Faith in South Africa*. Claremont: David Philip Publishers.

Goh, J. N. (2012) Mary and the Mak Nyahs. *Theology & Sexuality*, 18(3), pp. 215–233.

Goh, J. N. (2018). *Living Out Sexuality and Faith: Body Admissions of Malaysian Gay And Bisexual Men*. London: Routledge

González Ortuño, G. (2016) 'Sexual Dissidence, Faith and Release in Marcella Althaus-Reid', in Panotto, N. (Ed.) *Indecent Theologies: Marcella Althaus-Reid and the Next Generation of Postcolonial Activists*, pp. 87–104. California: Borderless Press.

Goss, R. E. (1993) *Jesus Acted Up. A Gay and Lesbian Manifesto*. San Francisco: Harper.

Goss, R. E. (1998) 'Sexual Visionaries and Freedom Fighters', in Gill, S. (Ed.) *The Lesbian and Gay Christian Movement: Campaigning for Justice, Truth and Love*, pp. 187–202. London: Continuum.

Henderson-Espinoza, R. (2015) 'Queer Theory and Latina/o Theologizing', in Espín, O. O. (Ed.) *The Wiley Blackwell Companion to Latino/a Theology*, pp. 329–346. Chichester: John Wiley & Sons.

Hirano, K. (2014) 'In Search of Dreams: Narratives of Japanese Gay Men on Migration to the United States', in Córdova Quero, H., Goh, J. N. and Sepidoza Campo, M. (Eds.) *Queering Migrations: Towards, From, Beyond Asia*, pp. 77–97. New York: Palgrave Macmillan.

Horie, Y. (2007) Possibilities and Limitations of 'Lesbian Continuum'. *Journal of Lesbian Studies*, 10(3–4), pp. 145–159.

Jordan, M. (2007) Religion Trouble. *GLQ*, 13(4), pp. 563–575.

Kelly, M. B. (2007) *Seduced by Grace: Contemporary Spirituality, Gay Experience and Christian Faith*. Melbourne: Clouds of Magellan.

Kelly, M. B. (2018) *Christian Mysticism's Queer Flame: Spirituality in the Lives of Contemporary Gay Men*. New York: Routledge.

Kornegay, E. (2012) Baldwin on Top. *Black Theology*, 10(3), pp. 328–338.

Kornegay, E. (2013) *A Queering of Black Theology: James Baldwin's Blues Project and Gospel Prose*. New York: Palgrave Macmillan.

Kuruvilla, P. (Ed.) (2017) *Christian Responses to Issues of Human Sexuality and Gender Diversity; A Guide to the Churches in India*. Bangalore/Delhi: CISRS/ISPCK.

Kwok, P-L. (2005) *Postcolonial Imagination and Feminist Theology*. London: SCM Press.

Kwok, P-L. (2010) 'Body and Pleasure in Postcoloniality', in Isherwood, L. and Petrella, I. (Eds.) *Dancing Theology in Fetish Boots: Essays in Honour of Marcella Althaus-Reid*, pp. 31–43. London: SCM Press.

Lightsey, P. R. (2012) Inner Dictum. *Black Theology*, 10(3), pp. 339–349.

Lightsey, P. R. (2015) *Our Lives Matter: A Womanist Queer Theology*. Oregon: Pickwick Publications.

Loughlin, G. (Ed.) (2007) *Queer Theology: Rethinking the Western Body*. London: Blackwell.

Nelson, J. B. (1979) *Embodiment*. Minneapolis: Augsburg Publishing House.

Nelson, J. B. (1988) *The Intimate Collection*. Philadelphia: The Westminster Press.

Nickoloff, J. B. (2003) Sexuality: A Queer Omission in U.S. Latino/a Theology. *Journal of Hispanic/Latino Theology*, 10(3), pp. 31–51.

Panotto, N. (Ed.) (2016) *Indecent Theologians Marcella Althaus-Reid and the Next Generation of Postcolonial Activists*. California: Borderless Press.

Punt, J. (2008) Intersections In Queer Theory And Postcolonial Theory, And Hermeneutical Spin-Offs. *The Bible And Critical Theory*, 4(2), pp. 24. 1–24. 16.

Robinson, M. (2015) 'Bisexual People', in Thatcher, A. (Ed.) *The Oxford Handbook of Theology, Sexuality and Gender*, pp. 640–656. Oxford: Oxford University Press.

Sneed, R. (2010) *Representations of Homosexuality: Black Liberation Theology and Cultural Criticism*. New York: Palgrave Macmillan.

Stuart, E. (Ed.) (1997) *Religion is a Queer Thing*. London: Cassell.

Sugirtharajah, R. S. (2004) 'Complacencies and Cul-de-sacs: Christian Theologies and Colonialism', in Keller, C., Nausner, M. and Rivera, M. (Eds.) *Postcolonial Theologies: Divinity and Empire*, pp. 22–38. St. Louis: Chalice Press.

Sweasey, P. (Ed.) (1997) *From Queer to Eternity. Spirituality in the Lives of Lesbian, Gay and Bisexual People*. London: Cassell.

The Nest Collective (2015), *Stories of Our Lives*. Nairobi: The Nest Arts Company.

Thatcher, A. (1993) *Liberating Sex. A Christian Sexual Theology*. London: SPCK.

Thoreson, R. R. (2014) Troubling the waters of 'a wave of homophobia': Political economies of anti-queer animus in sub-Saharan Africa. *Sexualities*, 17(1/2), pp. 23–42.

Tolbert, M. A. (1995) 'Reading for Liberation', in Segovia, F. F. and Tolbert, M. A. (Eds.) *Reading From This Place, Vol. I. Social Location and Biblical Interpretation in the United States*, pp.263–276. Minneapolis: Fortress Press.

van Klinken, A. (2013) *Transforming Masculinities in African Christianity: Gender Controversies in Times of AIDS*. London: Routledge.

van Klinken, A. (2015) Queer Love in a 'Christian Nation': Zambian Gay Men Negotiating Sexual and Religious Identities. *Journal of the American Academy of Religion*, 83(4), pp. 947–964.

van Klinken, A. (2017) 'Queer Studies and Religion in Contemporary Africa: Decolonizing, Post-secular Moves', *Scholar & Feminist Online*. Available at: http://sfonline.barnard.edu/queer-religion/queer-studies-and-religio n-in-contemporary-africa-decolonizing-post-secular-moves/2/

van Klinken, A. (2018) Autobiographical Storytelling and African Narrative Queer Theology. *Exchange*, 47, pp. 211–229.

van Klinken, A. and Chitando, E. (Eds.) (2016) *Public Religion and the Politics of Homosexuality in Africa*. Oxford: Routledge.

van Klinken, A. and Phiri, L. (2015) 'In the Image of God': Reconstructing and Developing Grassroots African Queer Theology from Urban Zambia. *Theology & Sexuality*, 21(1), pp. 36–52.

West, G., Van der Walt, C. and Kapya, J. K. (2016) When faith does violence: Reimagining engagement between churches and LGBTI groups on homophobia in Africa. *HTS Teologiese Studies/ Theological Studies*, 72(1). Available at: http://www.scielo.org.za/pdf/hts/v72n1/64.pdf

Williams, D. (1993) *Sisters in the Wilderness: The Challenge of Womanist God Talk*. New York: Orbis.

Yip, L-S. (2012) 'Listening to the Passion of Catholic *Nu-tongzhi*: Developing a Catholic Lesbian Feminist Theology in Hong Kong', in Boisvery, D. and Johnson, E. (Eds.) *Queer Religion: Homosexuality in Modern Religious History*, pp. 63–80. Santa Barbara: Praeger.

Zachariah, G. and Rajkumar, V. (Eds.) (2015) *Disruptive Faith, Inclusive Communities: Church and Homophobia*. Bangalore/Delhi: CISRS/ISPCK.

QUEER BIBLE

This chapter focuses on the act of reading and interpreting the Bible queerly. There are many exciting explorations in the field of queer biblical studies, where lesbian, gay, bisexual, and transgender interpretations offer innovative approaches to the Bible, as well as the methods of analysis which come from queer criticism. The first part of this chapter will examine the role of the Bible in terms of its influence and authority in queer theologies. The chapter then considers queer readings of the Bible from the position of non-normative sexual and gender identities. Moving onto explicit queer readings of the Bible, three approaches in queer biblical studies are discussed: (1) biblical hermeneutics and same sex relationships; (2) queering the Bible; and (3) queer ways of telling. Examples of queer readings are included throughout the chapter. Finally, attention is given to queer readings in global contexts, focusing on reader responses from Asian American, Asian, African, and Latin American contexts, as well as Black and womanist readings.

QUEERING AUTHORITY

Historically the Bible has played an important role in the development of society and culture. In today's society its influence is still prominent. Indeed, its authority is presumed in public life, as it is still used to swear an oath in court in many countries. In terms of the relationship between gender and sexual identities and the Bible in society, Deryn Guest notes how the Bible is 'a cultural artefact of considerable significance and influence, which is regularly deployed politically to bolster statements on such matters as transsexuality, civil partnerships, anti-discrimination law, gay adoption and parenting and so on' (Guest, 2012: 29). Its significance in the public sphere cannot be overestimated. Therefore, it is of great importance that biblical studies must engage with questions of sexual diversity and genderqueer identities.

Despite its influence on public, social, and cultural levels, the status and authority of the Bible is often misplaced in Christianity. Adrian Thatcher points out that the Bible does not claim to be the Word of God. He says, 'once the Bible is identified with the Word of God the text of scripture rivals or even replaces the Word of God, which is Jesus Christ' (Thatcher, 2008: 4). In such terms, Christians who elevate the status of the Bible to a point where it is worshipped commit bibliolatry – worship of the Bible instead of God. Thatcher warns how this, according to the Bible itself, is disastrous, as 'the letter kills, but the Spirit gives life' (2 Corinthians 3: 6). Moreover, there are arguments which state that the Bible cannot have any significance or authority for LGBTQ+ identified people. For example, Elizabeth Stuart says 'the Bible is the creation of the early church, a church whose patriarchal assumptions we no longer share. It can therefore have little authority for us, instead we need to develop a new canon of sacred writings which reflect our experience of God' (Stuart, 1997: 45).

It is clear so far that queer serves to disturb and disrupt. Queer biblical studies, therefore, place into question the status and authority of the Bible. More importantly, queer biblical studies offer transformative readings of biblical texts, and the queer Bible 'turns the Bible from being an enemy to a friend' (Stuart, 1997: 45). Timothy Koch advocates the process of queer reading as 'highly selective work' (Koch, 2006: 373), and explicitly refuses to allow traditional hermeneutics or church authority to decide on the meanings of the texts:

> we, as LGBT persons, come with our own questions, our own need for resources, our own limited energies; when we regard biblical texts as *resources* for us [...] We can find our own concerns, emotions, goals and fears reflected throughout these pages; we can find role models, cautionary tales, ribald stories and points to ponder that can illuminate our own journeys (Koch, 2006: 373).

LESBIAN, GAY, AND BISEXUAL THEOLOGIES AND THE BIBLE

Gay, lesbian, and bisexual readings of the Bible follow the lineage of feminist theology, which problematised the Bible. Derrick Sherwin Bailey, in his book *Homosexuality and the Western Christian Tradition* (Bailey, 1955), offered one of the first explorations into sexuality and Christianity. Bailey uses the term 'texts of terror' to refer to biblical passages which are used to condemn homosexuality. The terror is linked to fear of violence against homosexuals, especially given that the texts are often wielded as a weapon against LGBTQ+ people. For many LGBTQ+ people who are on the receiving end of pronouncements from such texts, this constitutes a form of spiritual abuse. Phyllis Trible was a pioneer in feminist biblical interpretation, exposing misogyny within scripture itself and also how this has resulted in misogyny by religious organisations. Using the same phrase as Bailey, Trible authored a book entitled *Texts of Terror* (Trible, 1984) where she published her ideas. Her work exposes how patriarchy in religion equates to misogyny, where women are subjected to oppression, abuse, and violence because of the interpretation of the scriptures. The idea of the 'texts of terror' was then applied to the biblical texts which are used to oppose same-sex relationships; as Goss states:

> The majority of Christian traditions believe that the Bible opposes homosexuality. The Bible has been used as a weapon of terror against gay men and lesbians. It has been interpreted to legitimize oppression against same-sex practices throughout Christian history. Biblical texts have been used by fundamentalist churches in their homophobic attacks upon gay men and lesbians in hate campaigns (Goss, 1993: 90).

One of the major considerations for gay and lesbian theology was how the Bible was used as a weapon to justify homophobic attitudes. The Bible is problematic, in this sense, and much work has been done to look at the original basis and contexts for the claims against same-sex relations. There are a number of biblical verses which are used by conservative Christians who condemn homosexual lifestyles and relationships. These have often been referred to as 'clobber texts', as they are commonly used to describe homosexuality as a sin. Here are some of the passages:

> Do not lie with a man as one lies with a woman; that is detestable. *Leviticus 18:22.*

> Because of this, God gave them over to shameful lusts. Even their women exchanged natural relations for unnatural ones. In the same way the men also abandoned natural relations with women and were inflamed with lust for one another. Men committed indecent acts with other men, and received in themselves the due penalty for their perversion. *Romans 1:26–27.*

> Do you not know that the wicked will not inherit the kingdom of God? Do not be deceived: Neither the sexually immoral nor idolaters nor adulterers nor male prostitutes nor homosexual offenders. *1 Corinthians 6:9.*

> They called to Lot, 'Where are the men who came to you tonight? Bring them out to us so that we can have sex with them. Lot went outside to meet them and shut the door behind him and said, 'No, my friends. Don't do this wicked thing. Look, I have two daughters who have never slept with a man. Let me bring them out to you, and you can do what you like with them. But don't do anything to these men, for they have come under the protection of my roof.' *Genesis 19:1–28 (Sodom and Gomorrah).*

Further examples exist in Leviticus 20:13, Deuteronomy 23:13, 1 Timothy 1:10, and 2 Peter 1:10. In asking the question 'what does the Bible say about...?', there is a hidden presumption that the definitive answer found in the Bible will carry authority or relevance. Yet biblical studies and biblical interpretation offer much more than being able to locate a biblical passage and claim bottom-line responses which are deemed to carry ultimate truth. Postmodern biblical studies bring into question the role, position, and power of the author, the text itself, and the reader, alongside engaging with critical theory and contemporary issues.

There are examples where the texts of terror are reshaped by offering reparative readings. In Nancy Wilson's publication of *Our Tribe: Queer Folks, God, Jesus and the Bible* (1995) she offers a space for biblical readings to be combined with a focus on experiences from lesbian, gay, and bisexual perspectives. Wilson describes the difference this project will make as follows:

> I believe that it is essential for gay men, lesbians, and bisexuals to take back the Bible. If we are not included among the stories and characters of the Bible, then it cannot be our book [...] Years from now, none of this will be shocking or unusual [...] As gay and lesbian biblical scholars come out, do the scholarship, and pay the price, the texts will be healed (Wilson, 1995: 164).

Wilson talks about cutting out the passages in the Bible which oppress. She underlines the fact that, throughout Christian traditional biblical interpretation, troublesome parts of the Bible are often glossed over or ignored, as gay and lesbian people engage in '"picking and choosing" only the parts of the Bible that support our point of view' (Wilson, 1995: 70). Yet those parts which are cut out, states Wilson,

> serve as very important reminders, as documentation of the history of oppression and the source of our struggles. They, too, are part of our tribal memory. For this reason – that *we may never forget* – it is still important for gay and lesbian people to understand how the Bible has been misused to oppress us (Wilson, 1995: 70).

Wilson speculates on the idea of there being a special place in hell for those who misuse the Bible in order to hurt or alienate others, acknowledging the irony in her own statement because she believes that hell does not really exist. Rather than think of the Bible as the divine Word of God, or as an untouchable and revered sacred text, Wilson states that the Bible offers a lot to speculate on. She describes an uncomfortable experience speaking on the theme of 'Outing the Bible' at her former college. The responses from her audience members were polite, yet hostile to her thinking. Her work exposes how it is a challenge to open up people's interpretive imaginations, as she writes 'it would be so much easier for these students if we gay and lesbians would just continue to hate ourselves and the Bible' (Wilson, 1995: 75). She refuses that position, stating: 'For me, the Bible is an elastic, resilient

friend who bounces back and even talks back when I question it [...]
The Bible belongs to anyone who will love it, play with it, push it to
its limits, touch it, and be touched by it – and the same is true for
God' (1995: 75).

How lesbian, gay, and bisexual Christians view the scriptures
sheds light on the question of authority of the Bible with regards
to religious identity. Sociologist Andrew Yip conducted some
pioneering research on the beliefs, attitudes, and lives of lesbian,
gay, and bisexual Christians (Yip, 2003). In one study, out of the
565 people questioned, 94.9% of gay men stated that the Bible
cannot be taken literally, while 96.2% of lesbians said the same.
Yip's study illuminates how, while 'the Bible was considered still
relevant to everyday life, it is nevertheless considered an insuffi-
cient guide for Christian living' (2003: 151). Similarly, Alex Toft's
work on bisexual Christians revealed that 87% of respondents
agreed that the Bible is often misinterpreted with regard to sexuality. That said, only 12% of bisexual Christians in his study
claimed the Bible was incompatible with modern life (Toft, 2009:
83). This points to the fact that bisexual Christians, like lesbian and
gay Christians, still feel that the Bible has relevance to them but
should not be taken literally, as it often is done in conservative
attitudes towards LGBTQ+ people. One of Toft's participants,
Adam, puts it as follows: 'It makes me so bloody angry that the
Church is hypocritical, and they will use this excuse of "well the
Bible says", and it's cherry picking' (2009: 84).

The pick 'n' mix approach to reading biblical texts is a popular
strategy among queer Christians. Melissa Wilcox calls this a 'biblical
buffet' strategy (Wilcox, 2002: 501). Her research with LGBT
Christians reveals how people take from the Bible what is relevant to
them, what pleases them, and they disregard anything which does not
appeal. One of the interviewees in her study is a bisexual man who
says just that: 'I take from the Bible what I can use, and I disregard a
lot of what I can't use' (2002: 501).

INTERSEX AND TRANS READINGS OF THE BIBLE

There are a number of biblical texts which enforce the distinction
between male and female identities, as well as those which blur
such distinctions. Genesis 1:27 states: 'So God created mankind in

his own image, in the image of God he created them; male and female he created them.' This verse has often been used to enforce the distinctions between the sexes in Christian belief. Conservative Christians may use the texts to point out that there seems to be no room for ambiguity in terms of gender. Sally Gross provides a closer reading of the Genesis 1:27 verse, and she says that the scripture should be read in context (Gross, 1999). According to Gross, the fact that Abraham and Sarah were unable to have children may reveal the possibility of Sarah's intersex body. Moreover, Gross is keen to mobilise the scriptural texts themselves to advocate for contemporary intersex bodies. Currently, many babies born into intersex bodies, where genitalia are ambiguous at birth, undergo medical procedures to align their genitalia with what are perceived as traditionally male or female bodies. There are many intersex activists who reject the idea of such surgery on young intersex bodies on the grounds that it is medically unnecessary, as the surgery is often cosmetic. There are arguments that such surgery is, in fact, genital mutilation. Gross says how scripture can support arguments against surgical interventions: 'biblical literalists should be persuaded by the letter of Scripture to be very suspicious indeed of genital surgery imposed upon intersexed infants when no intrinsic risk to life and physical health demands it. The removal of gonads and other such surgery is explicitly forbidden by Scripture (see Deut. 23.1, for example)' (1999: 74).

The presence of eunuchs in the biblical texts demonstrates the presence of intersex bodies within the scriptures. A eunuch was usually thought to be a castrated male or an individual with ambiguous genitalia. The verse from Deuteronomy 23.1 – 'No one who has been emasculated by crushing or cutting may enter the assembly of the Lord' – is an argument that can be raised to object to early surgery in intersex youth, but the argument is also applied by Christians who oppose sex reassignment surgery for trans people. There seems to be an obsession with emasculation and the erasure of male genitalia within such scriptures, and this is read alongside the numerous verses relating to male circumcision. There is a clear focus on the penis and its function to procreate, yet the scriptures do not give such attention to female genitalia for procreation. There are other positive references to eunuchs within the Bible:

> For this is what the Lord says: 'To the eunuchs who keep my Sab-baths, who choose what pleases me and hold fast to my covenant – to them I will give within my temple and its walls a memorial and a name better than sons and daughters; I will give them an everlasting name that will endure forever'. *Isaiah 56:4–5.*
>
> For there are eunuchs who were born that way, and there are eunuchs who have been made eunuchs by others – and there are those who choose to live like eunuchs for the sake of the kingdom of heaven. The one who can accept this should accept it. *Matthew 19:12.*
>
> As they travelled along the road, they came to some water and the eunuch said, 'Look, here is water. What can stand in the way of my being baptized?' And he gave orders to stop the chariot. Then both Philip and the eunuch went down into the water and Philip baptized him. When they came up out of the water, the Spirit of the Lord suddenly took Philip away, and the eunuch did not see him again, but went on his way rejoicing. *Acts 8:36–38.*

The texts demonstrate a more inclusive reading for intersex indivi-duals, and conservative Christians could still learn a lot from these texts! Yet a word of caution is needed. The verse from Matthew 19:12 shows variation in the reasons as to why people were eunuchs. Often castration was involuntary as eunuchs were slaves, and, although their presence was significant enough to be referenced in scriptural texts, there certainly did appear to be a lot of stigma around eunuchs in ancient times. The eunuch therefore becomes a symbol, an ancestor for queer people. Susannah Cornwall's work provides examples of how intersex people engage with such scriptures; as one of her participants, David, says:

> Of course I scoured the Bible to find out anything to do with intersex and I was thrilled when I discovered that Jesus spoke about it. My interpretation of what Jesus said about eunuchs ... I thought that was wonderful, yes. And that was the springboard for my faith. I thought, 'Jesus knows I exist! I'm not on my own'. Because I thought I was the only one in the world, you see (Cornwall, 2015: 225).

For transgender people there are texts of terror which can be used to bolster arguments against gender presentations and surgery. For example, Deuteronomy 22:5 prohibits cross-dressing: 'A woman must not wear men's clothing, nor a man wear women's clothing, for the Lord your God detests anyone who does this.' Such readings can be seen as another example where one of the 613 Hebrew laws are selected as important in Christian contexts while others are discarded. It is also an example where the verse can be counterbalanced by another scripture elsewhere in the Bible. For instance, in the New Testament there is a promise within the Bible that offers Christians a heavenly embodiment which defies binary gender. In Galatians 3:28, Paul writes, 'There is neither Jew nor Gentile, neither slave nor free, nor is there male and female, for you are all one in Christ Jesus'.

From a trans perspective, Mercia McMahon claims that the Bible is worse for transgender people than it has been for feminist theology. McMahon notes how there are no direct resources for transgender people within the Bible. They are able to look at texts – for example, the biblical eunuchs – and see elements that offer some evidence of gender variance, but she warns that these texts 'are rich virgins' as 'they do not fully equate to the experience of trans people' (McMahon, 2016: 66). Therefore, there is a need to look towards a trans reading of biblical texts. There are some emerging ideas in this area, as attention now turns to methods used in queer biblical studies.

QUEER APPROACHES IN BIBLICAL STUDIES

There are three main contemporary approaches to queer biblical scholarship. The first approach examines biblical hermeneutics with regards to same-sex relationships and works sensitively within traditional methods. The second approach looks at strategies used for queering the Bible, including the reception of the Bible by readers, who bring their own contexts and positions to it. The third approach is imaginative and creative, offering a retelling of the stories by recasting characters, events, plots, and contexts. Although they are discussed separately here for ease of explanation, these approaches are often combined and cross over.

[I] BIBLICAL HERMENEUTICS AND SAME-SEX RELATIONSHIPS

One of the first lenses in which queer readings of the Bible have troubled the idea of sexuality and gender has been through an analysis of linguistic and literary structures. This approach may also treat the Bible in the same as any other text of literature may be examined, focusing on language style, content, and genre. Trained scholars in ancient biblical languages have re-examined texts and their translations. For example, in 1 Corinthians 6:9–10 the Greek word translated as 'homosexuals' is *arsenokoitēs*. But this is an extremely difficult word to translate as it is composed of two parts – *arsen* (man) and *koite* (bed) – so 'manbedders' would be a rough fit. Some interpretations look at this word as referring to non-consensual sexual activity between men, such as rape, or an abuse of status and privilege from one man to another.

A second lens within this approach has been to examine the histories of the ancient contexts in which the texts were produced, demonstrating how radically different society and culture were. In biblical studies, the historical-critical interpretation of the Bible is a method which seeks to uncover the world behind the texts, exploring the histories and contexts of the time in which they were produced. Therefore, the method explores the themes of sexuality, gender, and examples of identity disruption in ancient contexts. The historical-critical method helps to create an under-standing of what life was like for the authors and characters in the stories. The writing of the ancient texts was a task carried out by those who were educated and therefore literary skilled. Authors of the biblical texts are privileged in some way, and their experiences and practices shape the texts. Generally, these privileged positions have resulted in the beginning of biblical traditions in which the narratives are cherished as divinely inspired.

Certainly, how we understand gender and sexuality today is radi-cally different from what would have been thought of at the times the texts were written. The sexual imagination was therefore very differ-ent. Nowadays there are sexual activities and discussions of sexual topics for which no explicit biblical reference exists, including, for example, discussions of pornography. The biblical texts pertaining to sexuality reveal how, in ancient times, the themes of marriage, rape, incest, and prostitution formed part of the laws on which Judaism, and later Christianity, viewed sexuality. Indeed, feminist biblical stu-dies have examined the patriarchy and power at play in how these ancient concepts have been upheld, to the detriment of women and sexually marginalised individuals.

Other interpretations which are found in queer hermeneutics include the positive same-sex relationships described in the biblical texts. The interactions between David and Jonathan and Naomi and Ruth become examples of same-sex relationships. It should be noted that scholars uncovering the positive focus on same-sex relationships use a literary reading of the texts. Therefore, exploring the narratives in this way does not expose David and Jonathan as a gay couple engaging in sexual acts, but points to the value of same-sex relationships.

> [1] After David had finished talking with Saul, Jonathan became one in spirit with David, and he loved him as himself. [2] From that day Saul kept David with him and did not let him return home to his family. [3] And Jonathan made a covenant with David because he loved him as himself. [4] Jonathan took off the robe he was wearing and gave it to David, along with his tunic, and even his sword, his bow and his belt. [5] Whatever mission Saul sent him on, David was so successful that Saul gave him a high rank in the army. This pleased all the troops, and Saul's officers as well. *1 Samuel 18:1–5.*

In 1 Samuel 16:18 we see how David is chosen for his good looks. Chapter 18:1 describes Jonathan's love for David as they become one in spirit. By Verse 3 this love is cemented in a covenant Jonathan makes with David – a commitment to one another in the form of a union. This text does not require a reader to have finely tuned gaydar to be able to see it as an example of same-sex commitment. The emotional attachment between the two men is undeniable, and the fact that their relationship was publicly condoned by the men in the army is significant.

Further on, in 2 Samuel 1:26, David grieves for Jonathan, saying, 'Your love for me was wonderful, more wonderful than that of women'. In 2 Samuel 6:20 David dances semi-naked before the ark of the Lord. This leads to disgust on the part of Michal, David's wife. Michal's repulsion lies in the fact that she has witnessed a series of relationships between David and Saul, then Jonathan, and now the Lord:

> David said to Michal, 'It was before the LORD, who chose me rather than your father or anyone from his house when he appointed me

> ruler over the LORD's people Israel—I will celebrate before the LORD. I will become even more undignified than this, and I will be humiliated in my own eyes ...' And Michal daughter of Saul had no children to the day of her death. *2 Samuel 6:21–23.*

Given Michal's annoyance and David's relationships with Jonathan and then the Lord, perhaps it is not too difficult to speculate on why she remained childless!

In the book of Ruth we see a similar intense and loving bond between Naomi and Ruth. Ruth is the daughter-in-law of Naomi. The text is pivotal in exploring the relationship and bond between the two women, which moves away from the backdrop of the male-dominated society and culture of ancient contexts where women were dependent on men. Marriage often equated to economic security and protection for women, and to some extent Boaz (Ruth's husband) offers a third element which helps to triangulate this bond in an economic sense. Yet there are no words of love or commitment between Ruth and Boaz, only Ruth and Naomi. The relationship demonstrates a same-sex loving commitment to one another:

> But Ruth replied, 'Don't urge me to leave you or to turn back from you. Where you go I will go, and where you stay I will stay. Your people will be my people and your God my God. Where you die I will die, and there I will be buried. May the LORD deal with me, be it ever so severely, if even death separates you and me.' *Ruth 1:16–17.*

Ironically, the statements of commitment and love between Naomi and Ruth are often used in heterosexual wedding ceremonies. Wilson notes the popularity of Ruth's declaration in heterosexual weddings and claims that 'these stories of committed faithful love, filled with risk taking, are moving, powerful biblical stories for gay and lesbian people. We must take them back' (Wilson, 1995: 156).

Similar stories exist elsewhere in the Bible; for example, the relationships between Mary and Martha and Jesus and Peter, among others, could be read with a queer eye. Yet sympathetic literary approaches to same-sex relationships do not focus on the physical expression of their love in any same-sex activity. Whether

David/Jonathan are gay, or Naomi/Ruth lesbian, we simply do not know. Wilson suggests that 'they could have had a deep platonic friendship that was also romantic in a homoerotic but not homosexual way' (Wilson, 1995: 156). In developing further the idea about sexuality and acting upon it, Guest highlights how focusing on this 'could play to the Church's game of distinguishing between a sexual orientation (which is acceptable) and acting upon it (which, in the case of homosexuality, is usually negatively evaluated)' (Guest, 2005: 185). Nonetheless, Guest rightly goes on to say that avoiding the possibility of genital acts actually offers a negative opinion of same-sex acts.

Exploring literal readings of same-sex relationships provides a way in for queering biblical hermeneutics; as Teresa Hornsby states, 'queer theory often enters a party on the arm of a more traditional guest' (Hornsby, 2006: 412). The limitations of a literary approach to same-sex relationships mean that the level of acceptability is drawn as long as the same-sex couples do not engage sexually. There is, of course, the potential to go beyond literary readings, and queer the texts even further, thereby offering the potential for more sexualised or intimate readings of the relationships. There is creative abundance in queering biblical studies in this way, which is discussed in both sections below.

[II] QUEERING THE BIBLE

In biblical studies the term *reception criticism* is used to refer to how the text is interpreted by the reader. The reader therefore makes their own meaning from the text that emphasises their own particular responses to it. Reception criticism can be thought of as a reader response. The Bible moves away from being considered as a timeless text with accepted and approved significance for all eternity. Instead it becomes part of a process in which the text is picked up by the reader who locates it in their particular contexts. The meaning is constructed in light of contemporary discussions.

Reception criticism looks at the impact the text has on an individual reader or reading community; in this method, the reception of the text becomes more important than the actual text itself. Perhaps only some aspects of the biblical text will be selected for discussion by the reader. Timothy Koch suggests a queer reader-response approach in which biblical texts are reinterpreted by 'cruising the scriptures' (Koch, 2001). Cruising refers to an activity where a person drives or walks around looking for a partner for sex, and it is a term popularised by gay culture. Cruising therefore offers a measure of excitement and a degree of risk. The risk is keeping an eye open for attackers or haters, while the excitement is located in the thrilling encounter with the text. Koch describes how biblical texts can be picked up according to tastes, connections, instincts, and experience. He says 'choosing to cruise means taking our own authority and responsibility for following up on whatever comes our way, for it is this which speaks to our desires' (2001: 175).

For queer biblical studies, the way in which LGBTQ+ individuals read and devise commentaries on the biblical texts in their own contexts results in lesbian, gay, bisexual, and transgender reception criticism. The most significant example of this is *The Queer Bible Commentary* (Guest et al., 2006). In this volume, each biblical text is not given verse by verse analysis, as is found in more traditional Bible commentaries, but portions of the text are selected which have relevance for the lives and interests of each commentator. Therefore, a queer commentary does not seek to offer answers to questions, but it offers creative, innovative, and empathic approaches to queer interpretation of scripture.

In order to examine the importance of queer reception criticism we are able to look at a few strategies offered by biblical scholars. Deryn Guest has been a pioneer in lesbian, queer, and trans biblical studies. In developing lesbian biblical hermeneutics, Guest advocates the principles of four Rs: resistance, rupture, reclamation, and re-engagement (Guest, 2005: 110), which are discussed below with reference to practical examples found in other queer readings.

RESISTANCE

Guest's work shows how reading texts with suspicion has been used in liberation, feminist, womanist, and postcolonial critiques. Guest offers a strategy of reading the text in a way which is suspicious of the presumed heterosexuality of the biblical characters and their relationships, *hetero-suspicion* (Guest, 2005: 124), and this can be mobilised for all non-normative gender or sexual identities. Reading in this way is an act of resistance. The method of hetero-suspicion encourages the reader to be suspicious of how heteronormativity and patriarchy have formed a bias in the texts themselves, and then in how the texts have been interpreted throughout history.

Examples of queer reception criticism which shows resistance and suspicion of the presumed heterosexuality of the characters include the stories of the relationships between David/Jonathan and Naomi/Ruth, as noted in the previous section. Another, more sexualised, example can be found in the reading of Moses in the book of Exodus by Rebecca Alpert (2006). She describes Moses as bisexual, in that he is married but is intimate with a male God. Alpert's reading looks specifically at the intimacy of the relationship between God and Moses. She points to the Jewish tradition where Moses was kissed by God and was called to have this special relationship with God. Alpert's commentary suggests how Moses and God's relationship becomes more sexually and erotically charged throughout the text, and therefore her reading demonstrates a commitment to a hermeneutic of hetero-suspicion, as suggested by Guest above. Alpert sexualises this hetero-suspicion, as Moses becomes 'the feminine, submissive partner who begs for God's attention, opens his orifice, and clings to God's rod' (Alpert, 2006: 71).

RUPTURE

Guest's second principle, rupture, focuses on how religious institutions and traditions have drawn upon certain biblical texts to enforce a binary of heterosexuality and homosexuality. The texts have been manipulated to demonstrate how one side of the binary, heterosexuality, is God-ordained. Similar to the use of the texts of terror, the other side of the binary, homosexuality, is used to indicate disapproval from God. As we have seen, the texts of terror have been re-examined using historical contexts and linguistic analysis to demonstrate how their reference to homosexuality is more nuanced than previously thought.

Guest's method of rupturing sex or gender binaries can be seen in further work on the 'transgender gaze' (Guest, 2016: 47). Guest states how 'the trans gaze in biblical studies is owned by those whose in-house knowledge and experiences provide the trigger for critical observation and insights' (2016: 57). Elsewhere in earlier work we see an example of a trans reading. Justin Tanis, self-identifying as a transsexual man, states 'it never occurred to me that God would not accept me, but I was very afraid that God's representatives within the Church might reject me' (Tanis, 2000: 44). Recalling the New Testament story of the woman at Canaan who approached Jesus to help heal her daughter, the disciples suggested Jesus should send her away. With a transgender gaze, Tanis reinterprets the story. His reception sheds light on contemporary concerns about non-binary gender people presenting in public. He ruptures the text by stating that 'the woman approaching Jesus to help her daughter was like a drag queen approaching a bunch of teenagers on a street corner to call 911 after her sister has been beaten' (2000: 45).

RECLAMATION

The third principle, of reclamation, works in conjunction with each of the other strategies, as Guest describes how a queer gaze operates on the scriptures, noting how the biblical texts often come alive for lesbian and gay readers. This allows for reclamation in the sense that the texts are then interpreted in ways which have not previously been explored, and this is a fundamental aspect of reception criticism. The Exodus is one story which has been reclaimed and re-interpreted in light of LGBTQ+ contexts. The book of Exodus describes how the Israelites were freed from slavery through the strength of God/Yahweh. Led by the prophet Moses, the Israelites were offered the promised land in return for their faithfulness. Mona West sees the process of coming out of slavery as similar to the process of coming out in the lives of LGBTQ+ individuals. West states, 'the themes of enslavement, exodus, wilderness wanderings, promised land, and exile parallel the stories of queer Christians who risk the security of their closets to find wholeness in relation to God and the believing community' (West, 2000: 73). The closet can be a secure environment; West highlights that coming out is not safe for everyone to do. So, rather than being an event which is celebratory, for some people it is an impossible task. West states: 'Queers die [...] often at their own hands when the only way out of the closet is suicide' (2000: 74). For those who are able to come out of the closet, there is a liberation similar to the Exodus story where LGBTQ+ people are able to affirm their own sexuality/gender and begin living authentically. In West's reading of Exodus, 'coming out, crossing over the boundaries of silence and homophobia, gay and lesbian Christians come home to God' (2000: 70).

RE-ENGAGEMENT

Guest's fourth strategy is to call for re-engagement with biblical texts. The emphasis here is on how the task is to exonerate or pardon scripture, to wrestle with scripture, and to reject the authority of the scriptures. In this way it has not been the scriptures themselves that have done wrong to LGBTQ+ people, but the finger of wrongdoing is pointed towards previous interpretations of the Bible in mainstream theology. Guest points to the need to study the actual texts themselves and to question the existing translations. According to Guest, this task means the scriptures themselves can no longer be harmful, as it blunts 'their capacity to kill by arguing it is the interpretation of the scriptures, not the scriptures themselves that have been condemnatory' (Guest, 2005: 247). Many individuals may use their own position to wrestle with the text itself. Guest notes that this is a place 'where one's inner conviction plays a pivotal role in discerning the priorities of the scriptures' (2005: 251).

The book of Lamentations is a bleak account of undeserved suffering. Guest's own reading of Lamentations sees the text as offering a voice to those who have suffered or been oppressed by the abuse of the Bible. Lamentations is an expression of anger, and Guest notes how the text offers a voice for the hurt caused by organised religion through homophobic and transphobic state-ments. Guest relates this to the experience of LGBTQ+ people in affirming their own sexual and gender identities. For those in churches that are not accepting or affirming of their gender or sexuality, Guest suggests that we follow the example of Lamenta-tions in which we are all 'invited to share in the expression of outrage and distress' (Guest, 2006: 403). Guest sees this anger as a pathway for LGBTQ+ people to negotiate their faith and to hold God and faith communities to account in their inclusion of LGBTQ+ people. This strategy of re-engagement is built on feminist theological thinking. Guest raises the question of allegiance and belonging for those who wish to remain faithful to their churches, asking 'is the continued effort to engage with scripture and one's religious tradition ultimately tantamount to collusion?' (Guest, 2005: 256). Those who remain within the tradition and uphold the authority of the scriptures could be accused of 'colluding' with the oppressor. Yet each individual has a right to make their own choices in relation to their feminist and religious allegiances. Having considered the principles of queer reception criticism and looked at various queer commentaries, we will now look at examples in which queer texts have been overhauled and rewritten using a queer lens.

[III] QUEER WAYS OF TELLING

So far we have seen how queer commentaries on the Bible offer both engagement with and disruption to the reading of texts. Queer readings have allowed LGBTQ+ people to resist, rupture, reclaim, and re-engage with the biblical texts, as noted in the previous section. A further approach in queer biblical studies is one in which the biblical texts are *queered*. To queer something means to disturb or to disrupt it, to turn it upside down. This approach allows for an entire imaginative retelling of the biblical texts using creative tools of writing. It allows for a style of biblical reading which is creative, original, and unique.

Within the field of queer biblical studies there are a number of examples to demonstrate how this queering works in practice. In one of the essays in *Queer Commentary and the Hebrew Bible* (2001), Roland Boer rewrites the entire relationship between God/Yahweh and Moses as one which is gay. In doing this he does not write an academic essay in the conventional style of traditional biblical writers, rather he writes the story in narrative prose. His essay begins with a playfulness of the biblical genre by including everyday situations. For example, on greeting one another, Moses says to Yahweh, 'big fucking mountain you've got here, Yahweh', to which Yahweh responds, 'Must impress the other gods, dear, can't let appearances slip' (Boer, 2001: 76) and then Yahweh makes tea for both men. There is adherence to some of the original biblical narrative in Exodus in terms of plot:

'Well', continues Yahweh, 'we need to have a chat, since I want you to make me a beautiful tent, a tabernacle where you and your Israelites can worship me.'
'Great, just what we need ...' begins Moses (Boer, 2001: 76).

Moving beyond features of the original storyline, we see further queer additions. Sexual tensions begin to emerge in their relationship and interaction in Boer's story, and Moses begins to see Yahweh as attractive. Later in the story, Boer narrates:

All this talk of tingling clothing, pomegranates and bells and hems, has made Moses horny; he is already at the half husky, dying for a look beneath those furs that Yahweh insists on wearing on this unbearably hot mountain. I'm sure he's got a great, pert, upright butt, he asserts (Boer, 2001: 78).

Queer theory, with its roots in postmodern thought, demonstrates how texts are not stable, and this includes the Bible. Mary Ann Tolbert notes 'how creatively and even joyously queer readers of the Bible reclaim some of its texts by destabilizing them, playing with them, laughing at them, allegorising them, tricking them' (Tolbert, 2000: ix). Elizabeth Stuart does exactly that, by encouraging a strategy of laughing in the face of scriptures used to oppress, such as the text of terror. She states, 'laughing at those texts is a strategy that subverts their efforts of destructiveness and distances us from the pain of being a target' (Stuart, 2000: 23). Retelling biblical stories in this way breaks down barriers between previous hostile and traditional interpretations in order to offer contemporary ways of reading and engaging with scripture.

Another queer way of telling is in James Martin's storytelling narrative of an encounter with Jesus. Martin tells the story of Jesus's appearance following the resurrection loosely, including a fictitious meeting between Jesus and a gay man. The encounter focuses on the love between the protagonist, Joseph, and Jesus. The story is told from the first-person perspective of Joseph. Jesus asks if he can meet Joseph's mother, and Joseph is hesitant as his mum considers him 'an abomination'. In Martin's telling of the story, Jesus is a faithful and encouraging friend who accompanies Joseph to confront this situation: 'as we walked along, and he pulled me close to him. He looked deeply into my eyes, as though he were looking into my soul, and he whispered to me again that everything would be fine' (Martin, 2000: 221). The queer retelling concludes, 'As I made my way home that evening, it all left me: all my fear, all my failings, all my self-doubt, all my embarrassment, all my pain, all the emptiness, all the loneliness, all of it was gone. His resurrection was my resurrection, you see. All because he loves me' (2000: 225).

One further example of the creative use of language in queer biblical approaches is in the use of Polari. Polari is considered a form of gay slang once used in the UK. It is a hybrid form of words from romance languages and London slang, and was often used by some in performance, at sea, and in gay subcultures. It is believed to be connected to Punch and Judy puppet performances, as they used Polari to converse. It is therefore fitting that the Bible has been rewritten in Polari by the Manchester Sisters of Perpetual Indulgence (more on the Sisters of Perpetual Indulgence in Chapter 5). It is available online at: http://www.polaribible.org/. Here is an example reading of the opening of Genesis:

1. In the beginning *Gloria* created the heaven and the earth.
2. And the earth was *nanti* form, and void; and *munge* was upon the *eke* of the deep. And the *Fairy* of *Gloria trolled* upon the *eke* of the *aquas*.
3. And *Gloria cackled*, Let there be *sparkle*: and there was *sparkle*.
4. And *Gloria vardad* the *sparkle*, that it was *bona*.

The retelling of texts clearly does not adhere to the traditional, established methods used in biblical studies, but that is the point of the queer project. Queer retellings disrupt the assumption that all characters are heterosexual and cisgender. Alternative tellings are possible. Queer approaches in biblical studies breathe fresh air into texts saturated in patriarchy, misogyny, and negativity towards same-sex relationships and transgender lives.

QUEER READINGS IN GLOBAL CONTEXTS

The Bible is a significant text that is read by individuals in various cultures and locations. As the missionaries brought Christianity to various places across the globe they also brought with them accepted interpretations of the Bible. Queer biblical studies must place such interpretations under a microscope and examine, disrupt, and expose them. Queer postcolonial biblical studies welcome voices from groups which have historically been marginalised in multiple ways. In the following sections we examine queer readings of the Bible in some global contexts. These include readings and interpretations given by LGBTQ+ individuals or a disruption of the texts based on the settings in which they are read.

ASIAN AMERICAN QUEER READINGS OF THE BIBLE

In his reading of Galatians in the *Queer Bible Commentary* (2006), Patrick Cheng describes his location as queer and Asian as 'a minority within a minority' (Cheng, 2006: 624). In this queer Asian reading, Galatians represents dominant white queer culture attempting to colonise those from minority ethnic backgrounds. In the letter to the Galatians, Paul talks about whether male followers of Jesus need to be circumcised or not, and he states that there is no need for circumcision. Cheng reframes the question, observing how compulsory circumcision is like compulsory heterosexuality and therefore not needed to be a Christian. He states how Galatians speaks powerfully to queer Asians, and he observes how the Gentiles' obsession with circumcision was similar to queer Asians who search for affirmation. He describes the alternative spiritual workshops he offers to gay men of Asian descent where they share and connect with one another's bodies.

In a short essay which reflects on the experiences of Asian Americans and the Bible, You-Leng Leroy Lim wonders 'Why folks don't just call themselves Holy Biblians instead of Christians?' (Lim, 2002: 316). Like Thatcher, Lim refers to how people state that the Bible is the Word of God, rather than Jesus Christ being the Word of God. Lim's essay is called 'The Bible Tells Me to

Hate Myself' and it recounts his experience as a university chaplain and his encounter with a young Christian man who had questions about homosexuality. The profound statement Lim uses as a title was the response a student gave to him when discussing faith. In pointing out how Asia is a vast continent – including India, Japan, and China – Lim appeals to religious leaders of Asian Christianity to blend the experience of Christianity with ancient wisdom practices of Asian traditions. Lim highlights the role of religious leaders in their use and abuse of the Bible, stating, 'the question is not about finding out which passages of scripture are relevant to Asian Americans, but what kinds of leaders and leadership qualities are needed by Asian Americans' (2002: 319), and pointing out that the Bible tells the story of a good leader.

ASIAN QUEER READINGS OF THE BIBLE

Missionaries used selective passages from the Bible in order to demonstrate how Christianity was superior to any local spiritual practices. Local expressions of religion were deemed uncivilised or inferior by the missionaries. One example of this use of the Bible is observed when the British occupied Hong Kong in 1842, and missionaries began to preach in the seaports.

Queer Asian readings of the Bible must pay due attention to LGBTQ+ lives and the Asian cultures and contexts in which the Bible is read. Joseph Goh explores its reception in Malaysia, where 9.2% of the population are Christian and where same-sex relations are illegal. The Christian churches there are widely disapproving of homosexuality, advising celibacy, counselling or conversion to heterosexuality for gay-identifying individuals. In his study of the Bible among non-heterosexual identifying men, Goh brings together biblical texts with the life-texts of sexuality (Goh, 2016). One of the participants, Artisan, sees the Bible as a message in which the idea of love surpasses any idea of disapproval or discrimination:

> Artisan: Ya ... you know that being a gay man is sinful in the mainline church context. And to me, is not, because on the bible, on John 3, 16 that for God so loved the world, and to me the world is inclusive of gay men, and not just straight men, certain sector of the society, is

the world ... every human being, is loved by God and I don't think, and I strongly believe that I'm not excluded at all [sic] (Goh, 2016: 45).

Another of Goh's participants, Skidiver, follows the verse in Leviticus 18:22 which prohibits a man from lying with a man as a man lies with a woman. In practice Skidiver says this does not prohibit sexual activity between consensual men, but that penetration should be avoided, as that is what he reads in the Leviticus reference. In his conclusion, Goh recommends that 'Christian communities and churches need to realize how important it is to confront, challenge and transform traditional interpretations of the bible' [sic] (Goh, 2016: 49).

In Chinese, the word *tongzhi* has been used to describe LGBTQ+ people, but without referring to a particular gender identity or sexual orientation. It also means 'comrade'. Kwok Pui-lan (Kwok, 2010: 35) notes how the term is almost similar to 'queer' in the west, but it is preferred in Chinese because it is different from the English word. She describes how homosexuality had been criminalised in Hong Kong through laws of sodomy inherited from British colonialism. In one example of queer Asian readings of the Bible, Tat-siong Benny Liew talks about Jesus's body in the gospel of John and describes it as 'cross-dressing' (Liew, 2009: 26). This reading of John's gospel aims 'to redress the wrongs suffered by people who have not been gendered strictly as male or female' (2009: 261). The text, therefore, comes alive for the gender-fluid, trans or intersex reader. Liew also states how John's gospel is queer as it recounts how Jesus is beaten, flogged, nailed, and pierced; he states how Jesus has 'a body that is being opened to penetration' (2009: 266). The text is queered in that Jesus's passion is positioned as a sexual encounter with a masochistic Father.

AFRICAN QUEER READINGS OF THE BIBLE

In Africa the Bible was introduced by missionaries who also brought along theological conservativism. Sub-Saharan Africa is now the global centre for Christianity, seeing a growth in church populations which are steadily declining in other countries. In the Anglican Communion, the Bishops of Africa are the strongest opponents to LGBTQ+ rights. The conservative attitudes from the western missionaries in Africa about sex and sexuality have now become so embedded that they are considered African values. This is often highlighted by those who are advocates for LGBTQ+ rights, recognising that conservative Christian values and readings of the Bible were a western import. In this way the argument that homosexuality is against African values becomes flawed and unconvincing, as we have seen in Chapter 3. The Bible is used as a justification to oppose LGBTQ+ rights, especially in the African countries in which homosexuality is illegal. The Bible has become a battlefield on which the question of LGBTQ+ rights is being fought against Christian conservatism.

Given such a culture of hostility, what methods do queer Africans use as they engage with the Bible? Queer African readings demonstrate a shift from institutional readings to individual interpretations. This means that queer African individuals are able to find their own meaning in the texts, rather than focusing on the authority of church bodies. The shift is indicative of general approaches to how LGBTQ+ people view tradition and scripture, as understandings of religion are personalised. This personalisation means that individual believers have direct access to texts and can construct their own interpretations and meanings.

Within Adriaan van Klinken's research on Christian Zambian gay men, all interviewees recognise God as love, and this is more important to their beliefs than scriptural readings. They worship God, rather than the text. One participant notes:

> Jesus Christ to me preached love, tolerance, hope, you know. That's what I chose to believe in, which is why I could embrace my Christianity and am not moved by what the Bible says about gay people ... You see people raising the Bible to say, 'God hates fags' – but the word 'hate' has never come out of the Lord's mouth. So they are the ones, those who are saying this, who are involved in blasphemy (van Klinken, 2015: 958).

An extensive study on the Bible and homosexuality in Africa, and specifically in Zimbabwe, was carried out by Masiiwa Ragies Gunda in 2010. Gunda states that it is not surprising that the majority of biblical scholarship on the question of sexuality has emerged from South Africa, as an African country with legislation in place to protect against discrimination on the basis of gender, sex, and sexuality. Focusing on the Bible as used by missionaries, Gunda points out a particular irony: the Bible was used by western missionaries to claim how many things in African culture were unbiblical, yet the Bible is used today by Africans to say how many things in western culture are unbiblical (Gunda, 2010: 36).

From a Kenyan perspective, stories of queer readings reveal how the Bible is seen as a tool to control people. Within *Stories of Our Lives: Queer Narratives from Kenya* (The Nest Collective, 2015), the section on spirituality and religion tells one story of a Christian who is unable to read the Bible because of the damage it does. One story says, 'Maybe there is another way of reading the Bible. I think the Bible is more than just a punishment structure for sinners' (2015: 302). Another story focuses on different biblical verses which can be used to empower queer people. Using the verse from Proverbs 13:20, one story writer says, 'walk with the wise and become wise, for a companion of fools suffers harm' (2015: 306). The idea of wisdom is linked to education, as several stories in the collection talk about reading widely and wisely, including philosophical texts or texts from other religious traditions.

LATIN AMERICAN QUEER READINGS OF THE BIBLE

There has been a trend in Latin American scholarship to use the biblical texts to advocate for social justice. This emerged during the time of liberation theology, where concern for the poor and marginalised was a focus. The marginalised of liberation theology did not include the sexually marginalised or women. The move beyond liberation theology to feminist and queer theologies began to recognise those excluded because of their gender, sex or sexual identities. Popular themes in Latin American biblical scholarship include liberation, postcolonialism, and the ideas of borderlands. In giving voice to the margins, these themes also serve to work with other queer approaches.

Fernando Candido da Silva (2012) observes how queer people have been excluded from Latin American biblical interpretations and he calls for an approach in which the queer community in São Paulo, Brazil, can re-examine 'the bible'. Da Silva calls for a use of lowercase 'b' when writing 'Bible' as this decreases its authority, and the text serves among many other spiritual writings used by queer folk. His idea of a queer community 'is based in multiple friendship networks, such as "families we choose"' [sic] (da Silva, 2012: 213). This community acknowledges differences but there is an alliance. Da Silva states how 'for the queer community the biblical text cannot represent supreme authority. This is, of course, a matter of survival' (2012: 214). Together, there is an awareness of the community, of its differences, and of the threat posed in reading 'the bible'.

The idea of a community reading of the Bible echoes the work of Latin American theologian Marcella Althaus-Reid. She thought of the act of theology and biblical engagement as a community project and called this a *caminata* (a walk). This requires a 'different engagement with the Bible, new questions concerning the patriarchal structures of sin needed to be unveiled in the Scriptures' (Althaus-Reid, 2004: 12). The structures relate to wealth, power, authority, and readings of the biblical texts. They also relate to gender, sex, and sexuality. A *caminata* allows for a different sort of engagement and this is a task done in solidarity with the community.

Focusing on Jesus's clothes in the gospel of Mark, Althaus-Reid locates him as one of the transvestites who is persecuted by Church and State. Jesus, dressed in royal purple and a crown of thorns, becomes the subject of laughter and mocking. This is similar to the transvestite in Buenos Aires or a Brazilian slum who 'attracts laughter and derision for her gender-fucking' (Althaus-Reid, 2006: 518). The story is retold within Latin American contexts of homophobia and transphobia. Althaus-Reid says that 'we need to read the life of Jesus with the same eyes that we read stories in the tabloids about homosexual people being killed. Unless we can locate Jesus' passion in the real life of people we will not be able to understand the meaning of incarnation nor the subversion of bodies that resurrection implies' (2006: 519).

Staying briefly with Mark's gospel, Oscar Cabrera uses reflections from Guatemala to re-read the story of Bartimaeus (Mark 10:46–52). Cabrera notes how Bartimaeus was excluded, yet he stands firm in his resistance. The crowd is loud and insensitive, trying to drown out Bartimaeus and other excluded voices. Cabrera states 'Jesus, who hears the voicing of the needy, restores the dignity that was snatched from Bartimaeus' (Cabrera, 2016: 251). Cabrera encourages Guatemalan theologians 'to think indecently, undisciplined, and in rebellious ways' (2016: 255).

BLACK/WOMANIST QUEER READINGS OF THE BIBLE

We have seen how the Bible has been used to support arguments against LGBTQ+ lives; conservative Christians often use the bottom-line response 'because the Bible says so'. Within the Black community it is not uncommon for Black preachers to be theologically conservative, having based their ministries on popular evangelical movements of the 20th century, such as that of Billy Graham. Graham made popular his repeated phrase about the authority of the Bible – 'God said it, I believe it, that settles it' – and this gives absolute authority to scripture. This common phrase, in use in Black churches even to this day, was consequently used to denounce LGBTQ+ identities and relationships. In her work on sexuality, Kelly Douglas notes how 'scripture is often the cornerstone of homophobia in the Black community' (Douglas, 1999: 90).

The Bible played a major role in the lives of African American slaves, who were often illiterate. The interpretation of the Bible was often what was handed down, and it was received without question. This meant that stories from the Bible which pointed to freedom caught the imagination of African American slaves. The Bible, therefore, offered hope, reflecting on stories where the oppressed are set free through faithfulness to God. The stories heard were used in prayers, spirituals, and testimony as they provided words which reflected African American experiences of struggle and survival. The Exodus story, describing the struggles and experience of the Israelites as slaves, served as a text which provided hope and comfort for African American people. It is a text which shows God's care and favour on those who are struggling or who are oppressed in some way. As many slaves were unable to access the Bible for themselves, they were unaware that there are biblical texts that serve to justify slavery. In contemporary society there is increased access to the texts as more people are literate and therefore able to read the stories for themselves.

Black and womanist queer readings of the Bible approach traditional interpretations with multiple suspicions. Given this double bind, why do Black and womanist queer people bother with the Bible at all? Pamela Lightsey notes how the Bible has been part of moral, social, and political life, especially as a large number of Black Americans belong to Christian religious traditions. She states, 'Scripture is not only a written instrument but also a way of life for many African Americans. We turn to the Bible for comfort, guidance and nurture' (Lightsey, 2015: 41).

CONCLUSION

The Bible is a significant source for Christian theology, and therefore queer theologies must disarm it of its potential to be used to hurt and abuse others. Queer biblical studies serve to re-examine and re-tell the Bible in the light of queer lives. Queer interpretations use queer identities to undercover how the texts speak to and for LGBTQ+ people. Queer biblical studies work with queer identities and queer theory. The Bible is disrupted and queered by focusing on gender, sex, and sexual identities which are not explicit in literal readings of the scriptures. When it has been used as a weapon to bolster arguments against LGBTQ+ lives and relationships, queer biblical readings allow the terror to be removed from scripture. This allows LGBTQ+ Christians of faith to be able to re-engage with the texts. As Tolbert says, 'When queers "take back the Word", we see within the Scriptures visions of hope and dreams of liberation' (Tolbert, 2000: 7). The queer Bible allows for freedom and prioritises the reader. Yet one final word of caution: queer readings of the Bible are multiple, creative, and have endless possibilities, but no queer reading of the Bible can become a stable or authoritative text. Queer means that all texts are unstable, as are all readers!

FURTHER READING AND ONLINE RESOURCES

Guest, D. (2005) *When Deborah Met Jael: Lesbian Biblical Hermeneutics.* London: SCM Press.

Guest explores the instability of the label 'lesbian' and offers significant elements which constitute a lesbian reading of scripture.

Guest, D., Goss, R. E., West, M. and Bohache, T. (Eds.) (2006) *The Queer Bible Commentary*. London: SCM Press.

A comprehensive commentary to the Bible with relevance for LGBTQ+ readers. Each book of the Bible is examined with a queer lens, offering fresh ways of looking at the biblical texts.

Thatcher, A. (2008) *The Savage Text: The Use and Abuse of the Bible*. London: Wiley-Blackwell.

An accessible, jargon-free book which exposes how the Bible has been used to discriminate against minority groups, including women, slaves, children, and people of colour.

http://www.oxfordbiblicalstudies.com/resource/lgbtq_Bible.xhtml

A website covering a reading of the Hebrew Bible by LGBTQ+ themes.

REFERENCES

Alpert, R. (2006) 'Exodus', in Guest, D., Goss, R. E., West, M. and Bohache, T. (Eds.) *The Queer Bible Commentary*, pp. 61–76. London: SCM Press.

Althaus-Reid, M. (2004) *From Feminist to Indecent Theology*. London: SCM Press.

Althaus-Reid, M. (2006) 'Mark', in Guest, D., Goss, R. E., West, M. and Bohache, T. (Eds.) *The Queer Bible Commentary*, pp. 517–525. London: SCM Press.

Bailey, D. S. (1955) *Homosexuality and the Western Christian Tradition*. London: Longmans.

Boer, R. (2001) 'Yahweh at Top: A Lost Targum', in Stone, K. (Ed.) *Queer Commentary and the Hebrew Bible*, pp. 75–105. London: Sheffield Academic Press.

Cabrera, O. (2016) 'A Postcolonial Reading of the Bartimaeus Story: Contributions Towards the Construction of Another Hermeneutical Model', in Panotto, N. (Ed.) *Indecent Theologies: Marcella Althaus-Reid and the Next Generation of Postcolonial Activists*, pp. 241–259. California: Borderless Press.

Cheng, P. S. (2006) 'Galatians', in Guest, D., Goss, R. E., West, M. and Bohache, T. (Eds.) *The Queer Bible Commentary*, pp. 624–629. London: SCM Press.

Cornwall, S. (2015) 'Laws "Needefull in Later to Be Abrogated": Intersex and the Sources of Christian Theology', in Cornwall, S. (Ed.) *Intersex, Theology, and the Bible. Troubling Bodies in Church, Text, and Society*, pp. 147–172. New York: Palgrave Macmillan.

da Silva, F. C. (2012) 'An Abominable and Perverted Alliance? Toward a Latin-American Queer Communitarian Reading of Deuteronomy', in

Brenner, A. and Yee, G. A. (Eds.) *Exodus and Deuteronomy*, pp. 205–236. Minneapolis: Fortress Press.

Douglas, K. B. (1999) *Sexuality and the Black Church*. New York: Orbis Books.

Goh, J. N. (2016) Survivalist sexuality-faith strategies in biblical meaning-makings: Non-heteronormative Malaysian Christian men and negotiations of sexual self-affirmation. *QUEST: Studies on Religion & Culture in Asia*, 1, pp. 38–53.

Goss, R. E. (1993) *Jesus Acted Up. A Gay and Lesbian Manifesto*. San Francisco: Harper.

Gross, S. (1999) Intersexuality and Scripture. *Theology & Sexuality*, 11, pp. 65–74.

Guest, D. (2005) *When Deborah Met Jael: Lesbian Biblical Hermeneutics*. London: SCM Press.

Guest, D. (2006) 'Lamentations', in Guest, D., Goss, R. E., West, M. and Bohache, T. (Eds.) *The Queer Bible Commentary*, pp. 394–411. London: SCM Press.

Guest, D. (2012) *Beyond Feminist Biblical Studies*. Sheffield: Sheffield University Press.

Guest, D. (2016) 'Modelling the Transgender Gaze', in Hornsby, T. J. and Guest, D. (Eds.) *Transgender, Intersex, and Biblical Interpretation*, pp. 45–80. Atlanta: SBL Press.

Guest, D., Goss, R. E., West, M. and Bohache, T. (Eds.) (2006) *The Queer Bible Commentary*. London: SCM Press.

Gunda, M. R. (2010) *The Bible and Homosexuality in Zimbabwe. A Socio-historical Analysis of the Political, Cultural and Christian Arguments in the Homosexual Public Debate with Special Reference to the Use of the Bible*. Bamberg: University of Bamberg Press. Available at: https://opus4.kobv.de/opus4-bamberg/frontdoor/index/index/docId/242

Hornsby, T. (2006) 'Ezekiel', in Guest, D., Goss, R. E., West, M. and Bohache, T. (Eds.) *The Queer Bible Commentary*, pp. 412–426. London: SCM Press.

Koch, T. R. (2001) 'Cruising as Methodology: Homoeroticism and the Scriptures', in Stone, K. (Ed.) *Queer Commentary and the Hebrew Bible*, pp. 169–181. London: Sheffield Academic Press.

Koch, T. (2006) 'Isaiah', in Guest, D., Goss, R. E., West, M. and Bohache, T. (Eds.) *The Queer Bible Commentary*, pp. 371–385. London: SCM Press.

Kwok, P-L. (2010) 'Body and Pleasure in Postcoloniality', in Isherwood, L. and Petrella, I. (Eds.) *Dancing Theology in Fetish Boots: Essays in Honour of Marcella Althaus-Reid*, pp. 31–43. London: SCM Press.

Liew, T-s. B. (2009) 'Queering Closets and Perverting Desires: Cross-Examining John's Engendering and Transgendering Word Across Different Worlds', in Bailey, R. C., Liew, T-s. B. and Segovia, F. F. (Eds.) *They Were All Together in One Place? Toward Minority Biblical Criticism*, pp. 251–288. Atlanta: Society of Biblical Literature.

Lightsey, P. R. (2015) *Our Lives Matter: A Womanist Queer Theology*. Oregon: Pickwick Publications.

Lim, Y-L. L. (2002) 'The Bible Tells Me to Hate Myself': The Crisis in Asian American Spiritual Leadership. *Semeia*, 90–91, pp. 315–322.

Martin, J. (2000) '"And Then He Kissed Me": An Easter Love Story', in Goss, R. and West, M. (Eds.) *Take Back the Word: A Queer Reading of the Bible*, pp.219–226. Cleveland: Pilgrim Press.

McMahon, M. (2016) 'Trans Liberating Feminist and Queer Theologies', in Beardsley, C. and O'Brien, M. (Eds.) *This is My Body. Hearing the Theology of Transgender Christians*, pp. 59–68. London: Darton, Longman and Todd.

Stone, K. (Ed.) (2001) *Queer Commentary and the Hebrew Bible*. London: Sheffield Academic Press.

Stuart, E. (Ed.) (1997) *Religion is a Queer Thing*. London: Cassell.

Stuart, E. (2000) 'Camping around the Canon: Humour as a Hermeneutical Tool in Queer Readings of Biblical Texts', in Goss, R. and West, M. (Eds.) *Take Back the Word: A Queer Reading of the Bible*, pp. 23–34. Cleveland: Pilgrim Press.

Tanis, J. (2000) 'Eating the Crumbs that Fall from the Table: Trusting the Abundance of God', in Goss, R. and West, M. (Eds.) *Take Back the Word: A Queer Reading of the Bible*, pp. 43–56. Cleveland: Pilgrim Press.

Thatcher, A. (2008) *The Savage Text: The Use and Abuse of the Bible*. London: Wiley-Blackwell.

The Nest Collective (2015) *Stories of Our Lives. Queer Narratives from Kenya*. Nairobi: The Nest Arts Company.

Toft, A. (2009) 'Bisexual Christians', in Hunt, S. (Ed.) *Contemporary Christianities and LGBT Sexualities*, pp. 67–86. Surrey: Ashgate.

Tolbert, A. M. (2000) 'Foreword', in Goss, R. and West, M. (Eds.) *Take Back the Word: A Queer Reading of the Bible*, pp. vii–xii. Cleveland: Pilgrim Press.

Trible, P. (1984) *Texts of Terror: Literary Feminist Readings of Biblical Narratives*. London: SCM Press.

van Klinken, A. (2015) Queer Love in a "Christian Nation": Zambian Gay Men Negotiating Sexual and Religious Identities. *Journal of the American Academy of Religion*, 83(4), pp. 947–964.

West, M. (2000) 'Outsiders, Aliens, and Boundary Crossers: A Queer Reading of the Hebrew Exodus', in Goss, R. and West, M. (Eds.) *Take Back the Word: A Queer Reading of the Bible*, pp. 71–80. Cleveland: Pilgrim Press.

Wilcox, M. (2002) When Sheila's a Lesbian: Religious Individualism among Lesbian, Gay, Bisexual, and Transgender Christians. *Sociology of Religion*, 63(4), pp. 497–513.

Wilson, N. (1995) *Our Tribe: Queer Folks, God, Jesus and the Bible*. San Francisco: Harper Collins.

Yip, A. K. T. (2003) Spirituality and Sexuality: An Exploration of the Religious Beliefs of Non-Heterosexual Christians in Great Britain. *Theology & Sexuality* 9(2), pp. 137–154.

5

QUEER THEOLOGIES FROM QUEER LIVES

There seem to be two main concerns in the production of queer theologies: the first focusing on issues of non-normative sexuality, representing LGBTQ+ people from where the term 'queer' emerged; and the second moving beyond identity or being anti-identity, as a critical approach. There are a number of scholars concerned with the idea that queer theologies are an intellectual project, rather than an activity that looks at the negotiations and renegotiations of queer lives in Christianity. Of course, as an academic area of study, queer theologies are rich in terms of the intellectual gains which come from studying queer theory and theology. But what about LGBTQ+ Christians? The lines between theologies of non-normative sexualities and queer theologies have been blurred. Within queer theologies there still needs to be space to explore bottom-up theologies that emerge from queer people. Many people who come to study queer theologies do so precisely because of their own self-identification, personal location or a commitment to issues of social justice in gender and sexuality. Indeed, attention must be paid to individual lives; as Marcella Althaus-Reid states, 'it is from human sexuality that theology starts to search and understand the sacred, not vice-versa' (Althaus-Reid, 2000: 146).

Before we consider queer theologies that emerge from queer lives, we should first look at the relationship between the churches and LGBTQ+ people. In addition to discussing the academic literature relating to queer theologies from life stories, this chapter briefly engages with the body of literature relating to religion and LGBTQ+ sexualities in the academic discipline of sociology of religion. Most importantly this chapter offers insights into the genuine life experiences of LGBTQ+ Christians, including lesbian, gay, bisexual, trans, and intersex voices. Attention is also given to the following 'queer' theologies of sexuality: asexuality, celibacy, 'straight' queers, kinky Christians, and the order of queer nuns known as the Sisters of Perpetual Indulgence.

THE CHURCHES' POSITIONS

The churches' positions on non-normative gender and sexuality have caused controversial debates across the mainstream Christian denominations. Within the Anglican Communion there are rifts between more progressive voices (situated largely in the global west) against the conservative voices emerging predominantly from Africa, which has become the home of the Christian centre. An analysis of the pronouncements and debates relating to LGBTQ+ lives from all main denominations is beyond the scope of this chapter, but to highlight the impact of the churches' positions in relation to gender and sexuality I consider briefly two mainstream denominations: the Roman Catholic Church and the Anglican Communion. In this discussion, 'homosexuality' is the language used by the official Church documents to refer to same-sex attraction. It is widely acknowledged that this use of language is outdated, with 'gay', 'lesbian', 'bisexual', and 'same-sex' being more commonly used. One of the reasons for such archaic language is that the churches have not moved from their original positions or pronouncements.

The Roman Catholic Church is based in Rome, as its name suggests. It is headed by the Pope and is the oldest of Christian institutions. There is no official doctrinal position from the Roman Catholic Church in relation to transgender, although sex assigned at birth is equated with gender. In terms of same-sex attraction, the situation is more complex as the Roman Catholic position declares that to have an inclination towards homosexuality is not a sin, but 'it is a more or less strong tendency ordered toward an intrinsic moral evil and thus the inclination itself must be seen as an objective disorder' (Congregation for the Doctrine of the Faith, 1986). This idea of 'disorder' has echoes to past ideas about homosexuality being a psychological disorder. The American Psychiatric Association took homosexuality off its list of disorders in 1987, while the World Health Organization only removed homosexuality from its classification of disorders in 1992. We see how the Roman Catholic position in 1986 uses similar language and has not been updated or revised since.

The Roman Catholic position, therefore, recognises that people have an inclination towards homosexuality and this is not a sin, but acting on this inclination and having same-sex relationships is sinful. Gay, lesbian, and bisexual people therefore should not engage in same-sex activities and are called to celibacy. The Roman Catholic Church calls for people not to discriminate, as the doctrine also says, 'Such persons must be accepted with respect, compassion and sensitivity. Every sign of unjust discrimination in their regard should be avoided' (Catechism of the Catholic Church, 1993).

The Roman Catholic Church does not recognise or celebrate same-sex marriage. In 2003, in the publication of 'Considerations Regarding Proposals To Give Legal Recognition To Unions Between Homosexual Persons', we can see further examples of the Church reiterating its position:

> There are absolutely no grounds for considering homosexual unions to be in any way similar or even remotely analogous to God's plan for marriage and family. Marriage is holy, while homosexual acts go against the natural moral law. Homosexual acts close the sexual act to the gift of life. They do not proceed from a genuine affective and sexual complementarity. Under no circumstances can they be approved (Congregation for the Doctrine of the Faith, 2003).

The Vatican's position on ordaining even celibate gay-identifying men was clarified in 2005 with the document 'Instruction Concerning The Criteria of Vocational Discernment Regarding Persons With Homosexual Tendencies In View Of Their Admission To Seminaries And Holy Orders'. The document, authorised by former Pope Benedict XVI, states how the Church 'cannot admit to the seminary or to holy orders those who practice homosexuality, present deep-seated homosexual tendencies or support the so-called "gay culture". Such persons, in fact, find themselves in a situation that gravely hinders them from relating correctly to men and women'. The Roman Catholic Church has not updated its official positions to date, and such doctrines are hostile to the lives of

LGBTQ+ people. Moreover, these positions have psychological and emotional effects on LGBQT+ Christians who seek to reconcile their non-normative gender/sexuality with their religion.

The situation in the Anglican Communion is a little more nuanced. The Anglican Church came into being when Henry VIII separated the Church from Rome in England. The Anglican Communion is how it has come to be known, a group of world-wide churches historically based on the Church of England. The Communion is diverse, and the large majority of its members are currently in the global south, namely Africa, where it is experiencing growth – yet in the global west there is decline in the number of people claiming to identify with Anglicanism. The diverse populations across the globe reflect the differences of opinions among its churches regarding the question of homosexuality.

The current position of the Anglican Communion comes from a conference held by its leaders in 1998, called the Lambeth Conference. The Anglican leaders voted on the issue of same-sex marriage, and the conclusion of this conference was that homosexuality 'is incompatible with Scripture'. It affirms traditional Christian teaching that marriage is between one man and one woman. Article 1.10 from the Resolutions Archive deals with the issue of human sexuality. The positional statement is that the Anglican Communion:

- reaffirms the traditional teaching upholding faithfulness between a husband and wife in marriage, and celibacy for those who are single;
- notes that the Holy Scriptures are clear in teaching that all sexual promiscuity is a sin, is convinced that this includes homosexual practices between persons of the same sex, as well as heterosexual relationships outside marriage;
- respects as persons and seeks to strengthen compassion, pastoral care, healing, correction and restoration for all who suffer or err through homosexual or other kinds of sexual brokenness (Anglican Communion Office, 1998: 10).

Similar to the Roman Catholic Church, the Anglican Communion adopts an approach which expresses empathy for those who experience same-sex attraction. The records contain a statement to this effect, that it:

calls on all our people to minister pastorally and sensitively to all irrespective of sexual orientation and to condemn irrational fear of homosexuals ... We commit ourselves to listen to the experience of homosexual persons and we wish to assure them that they are loved by God and that all baptised, believing and faithful persons, regardless of sexual orientation, are full members of the Body of Christ (Anglican Communion Office, 1998: 9).

In terms of bisexuality, Anglicanism teaches that Christians who are bisexual must 'choose' to be either celibate or straight. The House of Bishops states, 'if God's overall intention for human activity is that it should take place in the context of marriage with someone of the opposite sex, then clearly the Church needs to encourage bisexual people who are capable of entering into such a relationship to do so' (House of Bishops, 2003: 283).

The resolution at Lambeth in 1998 is not legally binding for the churches, however, and the nature of 'common faith' in baptism is what unites the Anglican Communion. That means there is huge variation in the practices among the churches which form its membership; from churches that do not accept LGBTQ+ individuals, to accepting and inclusive churches that are happy to welcome same-sex partnered people who are not celibate. Of course, lesbian, gay, bisexual, and transgender people comprise some of the church ministers and leaders. The issue and differences of opinion between the churches belonging to the Communion have led to controversial discussions of rifts between the union of churches.

The current position of the churches certainly points to a general hostility towards LGBTQ+ people. There is a risk that the position of the churches becomes the dominant voice in discussions of LGBTQ+ persons and Christianity. I agree with Colby Dickinson and Meghan Toomey who state how queer theologies decentre 'the "standard" patterns of theological talk, not to centralize itself within this dialogue. One way it accomplishes this is by continually shifting focus onto the real persons and lives that exist at the margins of both society and Christianity' (Dickinson & Toomey, 2017: 3). In such a climate, how do LGBTQ+ people live out their Christian faith with their gender and/or sexuality?

LIFE STORIES AS QUEER THEOLOGIES

> There is an embarrassed reluctance to listen to alternative stories about sex ... because of the substantial investment of hetero-patri-archy among powerful parts of church and society (Nixon, 2008: 613).

David Nixon reveals how paying attention to life stories as a source for theology moves away from institutions which maintain het-eronormative and patriarchal structures. There is, therefore, a reluctance to listen to the hurt and damage these structures have caused to individual lives. In this context, this chapter focuses on contextual queer theologies, grounded in the lives, beliefs, and practices of non-normative individuals. By 'non-normative' I refer to people whose self-identifications and/or sexualities do not align with traditional Christian understandings of gender and sex. What are considered 'non-normative' identities are pitted against reli-gious beliefs and doctrines, and there is a perception that Chris-tianity is hostile to non-normative individuals and groups. At one end of the spectrum there is the extremist homophobic language used by Westboro Baptist Church, which uses banners proclaiming how 'God hates fags'. In the middle are the positions of church authorities, as noted above, which result in continuous, complex, and controversial conversations. Happily, at the other end of the spectrum we see how many Christians on the ground, in various denominations and contexts, are working towards welcoming and even celebrating LGBTQ+ individuals.

The injunction for life-story research as a source of theology emerges throughout the literature in the sociology of religion and queer theologies. Althaus-Reid states, 'At the bottom line of queer theologies, there are biographies of sexual migrants, testimonies of real lives in rebellions of love, pleasure and suffering' (Althaus-Reid, 2003: 8), and some of that suffering has come at the hands of the churches, as well as widespread prejudice and discrimination. To explore queer theologies further we must begin to look at the testimonies and life stories of queer Christians. Of course, life-story research is contextual, as illustrated through queer theologies in global contexts in Chapter 3. In early gay and lesbian theology the themes of conflict and reconciliation demonstrate tensions between the religious and sexual identities of lesbian and gay people.

Institutional forms of religion and use of the Bible to condemn same-sex relations meant that many lesbian, gay, and bisexual people experienced inner emotional conflict in an attempt to wrestle with their religious and sexual identities. The psychological impact and damage done by churches and the misuse of scripture is widespread. Michael Ford notes how 'Christ may have said that the truth sets people free, but for many homosexuals, including those in the church, the fear of their own self-identity keeps them locked in psychological captivity' (Ford, 2004: 11).

In *Undoing Theology: Life Stories from Non-normative Christians,* I examine the rich potential in producing queer theologies from the sharing of life stories and experiences (Greenough, 2018). There are five major outcomes from producing queer theologies from our own sexual and gendered experiences: '(i) stories are transformative because they are relational; (ii) stories can help individuals make sense of their lives; (iii) stories are messy; (iv) stories disrupt the binary between material and divine; (v) stories have the potential to mark and queer heterosexuality' (2018: 26). The act of sharing our experiences means we are no longer isolated. Our stories are punctuated with our feelings and emotions, as personal and subjective as they may be. Telling our experiences to others is a relational task – we share vulnerability and are affirmed by others. Human experiences are messy, so the telling of our stories is something which is also messy as it is based on memory, selection, and the constant reinterpretation of life experiences. When our life experiences become stories to do with our faith, they become testimonies. These stories also complement scripture as sacred stories. Moreover, queer theologies are not something produced solely by LGBTQ+ people, but queer heterosexuals exist, as I discuss in a later section.

In the example of life-story research from *Undoing Theology,* I explore the spiritual and religious journeys of three protagonists, each of whom choses a pseudonym. The aim is to listen to the queer theologies that emerge, and the process of 'undoing' allows people to renegotiate their faith based on their life experiences. Religious identities, like all identities, are not fixed. Life stories are a source for queer theologies as they value the potential of personal, experiential theologies which allow people to transform their understanding of Christianity. The narrative chapters offer bottom-up queer theologies from Alyce, an intersex identifying Catholic; Caddyman, a former leader of 'ex-gay' conversion therapy in the USA; and Cath, a heterosexual woman who practises acts of bondage and submission. The aim of 'undoing theology' is therefore to focus on how the protagonists have negotiated traditional theology in light of their experiences. The process of 'undoing' means that an individual's religious and spiritual identities are not static. They evolve and change over the course of our lifetimes, as queer theory exposes how identity is not stable in any case. This allows us to reconceptualise different elements of Christianity based on our self-awareness and self-identifications. Stories we tell about ourselves, our lives, our beliefs actually change and evolve – therefore theologies are temporal.

Theologies from individual lives expose how God has been constructed as fixed in traditional theology, whereas the very nature of God is unfixable, uncapturable, and unpredictable. By 'undoing' God we free the divine from bondage, which has been repeated through rigid, traditional theological frames. Looking at experience and life stories adds colour and diversity to theology, but it does have its own limitations too. One of the cautions is that we end up making God in our image, rather than humans being made in the image of God. It is important that non-normative Christians use their own voices to tell of the damage done by Christianity and its policing of gender and sexuality, but also to preserve what is good in Christianity within their lives.

QUEER LIVES AND SOCIOLOGY OF RELIGION

Sociology of religion is the academic area which focuses on how religion functions in society. Aside from work done in theology and religious studies, extensive work on LGBTQ+ Christians – their beliefs and lives – has emerged in sociology. Within the area of sociology of religion, extensive and ground-breaking research has been conducted in the following areas: Andrew Yip's pioneering work on gay male Christians (Yip, 1997) and further work on LGBT identities and spiritualities (Yip, 2000, 2002, 2003); Alex Toft's work on bisexual Christians (Toft, 2009, 2014); and Melissa Wilcox's research with lesbian, gay, bisexual, and transgender Christians (Wilcox, 2002, 2003, 2009).

Research into the lives of gay, lesbian, and bisexual Christians was carried out by sociologist Andrew Yip. He collected data from 565 gay, lesbian, and bisexual Christians who completed a 17-page questionnaire regarding their religious beliefs, and then he interviewed 61 respondents. The results of the project were widely published. The research project covered a large section of those within mainstream denominations – Church of England (48%), Roman Catholic (26.4%), and Methodist (29.5%) (Yip, 2003: 141). Yip's analysis of the data demonstrates how 'most respondents saw no conflict between their sexualities and their Christian faith' (2003: 137) and concludes that 'the majority of respondents appeared to have developed positive self-identities that harmoniously incorporated their stigmatised sexualities and Christian faith' (2003: 137). Yip's research shows how, at the turn of the millennium, lesbian, gay, and bisexual Christians were able to reconcile faith with their sexualities. As part of his study Yip asked his participants about sources of authority in their faith, including church and the Bible. He asked respondents to rank, in order of importance, four ideologies considered core elements to Christian faith: personal experiences, the Bible, human reason, and church authority. Overwhelmingly, the majority of non-heterosexual Christians (81.9%) ranked 'personal experience' as the basis of their faith (Yip, 2002: 207). His research demonstrates that non-heterosexual Christians personalise their faith, rather than relying on sources of authority such as the church or the Bible. One of his participants, Kim, states:

> I certainly know why I put church authority at the bottom. That's because of my attitude to the church. The reason I put personal experience on the top is that any Christian will tell you that their relationship is about their personal experience of god. That's the same with me. When people talk to me about Christianity, the only way I can relate it to them is to talk about my own personal experience of god, and how my life has changed as a result of coming into contact with god. That would never have happened by the church authority telling me god existed. Having encountered god, my own reasoning told me that there was god. The bible, in a sense also backs up what I have experienced. So yes, it is my reasoning and my reading of the bible, in relation to my experience, not what the church has to say [sic] (Yip, 2002: 206).

In addition to collecting rich data and snippets of interviews throughout his work, Yip places emphasis on the importance of life-story research:

> Accompanying the development of social scientific literature is the emergence of anecdotal narratives and personal biographies [...] The importance of such writings cannot be denied. They often offer moving and powerful stories of courage, resilience, and wisdom. In many ways, they could be more effective than scholarly writings precisely because they are not wrapped in academic language (Yip, 2010: 48).

Inclusive church congregations, such as the Metropolitan Community Church (MCC), welcome lesbian, gay, bisexual, and trans Christian worshippers. In a study of these congregations, Wilcox highlights that the vast majority of congregants are male. She asks, 'Where are all the women?' (Wilcox, 2009: 5). Wilcox goes in search of the queer women in order to explore their experiences of spirituality and faith across a wide range of religious institutions, such as mainstream churches, liberal synagogues, LGBT welcoming and affirming congregations, as well as alternative spiritual practices such as contemporary paganism. This shows the variety of religious practices across a broad spectrum of people, but Wilcox also explores the motivating factors that lead to the religious practices. She highlights how queer women exercise choice, resulting in a religious individualism which is based on their own experiences rather than institutional membership. This issue of choice in an open religious market for LGBT individuals was the subject of her sociological inquiry into 72 members of MCC. In terms of theology, the participants' understanding of God was wide and varied; as Wilcox says, 'for some, God is a father; others think of God as "parent" or "mother/father." And some spoke more loosely of an energy, a flow, a life force, the Universe' (Wilcox, 2002: 506).

Bisexual individuals are often under-researched, and particularly so in terms of their religious identities. Bisexual identities are often conflated under lesbian or gay ones, or there is a common view that bisexual people can 'pass' as straight. Wilcox notes how it is dangerous to combine the experiences of lesbian, gay, bisexual, and trans as one grouping because the 'challenges faced by members of LGBT communities differ not only because of gender identity or sexual orientation, but also because of biological sex, race, ethnicity' (Wilcox, 2003: 30). The reason they are grouped as a community is that collectively each identity challenges traditional concepts of gender and sexuality in traditional Christianity. In the area of sociology of religion, Toft has produced some much-needed pioneering work to investigate the lives of bisexual Christians. He notes how 'bisexuality becomes invisible because it sits in the middle of both homosexuality and heterosexuality' (Toft, 2014: 551). His study involved 80 participants identifying as bisexual completing questionnaires, with 20 follow-up interviews. Only 40% of his respondents thought that their bisexuality allowed them to fit into both heterosexual and homosexual communities (2014: 560). Toft explores what the churches say about bisexuality and then he looks at how his participants challenge this in some way. He notes how the churches view bisexuality simply as sexual activity, rather than a sexual identity with its own capacity for relationships. Examples of theologies formulated by his participants include that of Rose, who looks at how Jesus related to others and this informs her bisexuality: 'It is based on his works, what he did for people, not just sex … being open with people and not seeing people as just a man or a woman. Just seeing people as people I guess. He would have been bisexual because of how he related to people' (2014: 558). Another participant, Phillip, sees God in everyday life. He says, 'You walk down the street and there is God. I don't find that in the programme of the Church. I read the Bible and the gospels and that seems to be what Jesus was about, just wandering around, outside the structure of religion. Actually talking to people about the world' (Toft, 2009: 80).

The work conducted by the sociologists of religion explores the living experiences, beliefs, and practices of LGBTQ+ Christians. The work provides a voice for people to say how their experiences within the churches have led to a rejection of institutional forms of religion. By focusing on their own experiences, including their gender and sexual identities, they personalise their own faith and express it in individual ways.

THEOLOGIES OF TRANS LIVES

Trans is a term used to refer to transgender people as a collective group, but there are some more accurate terms to use. A transman is someone who was assigned female at birth but transitions to live as a man. A transwoman is someone assigned male at birth but transitions to live as a woman. Trans itself literally means 'beyond' or 'across'. The process of transition may be a social process, in which a transperson presents in their new gender in daily life, or a physical process, which may involve gender reassignment surgery. A transperson is trans whether they have transitioned either socially, physically or both. That's to say, surgery is something which individual transpeople may choose for themselves, but it is a personal and private choice. Using the correct pronouns to describe transpeople is really important to recognise their gender presentations. Some may adopt the pronouns of their transitioned gender, and other pronouns such as 'ze, zir, hir, zirself' are also used as non-binary terms. It is common for some transpeople to adopt the pronoun 'they' in the singular to avoid using 'he' or 'she'. A person may choose to self-identify as 'agender', which means they do not adopt binary gender labels. 'Bigender' refers to someone who identifies as male and female, and presents gender according to choice or their setting. There are other terms used by people to reject gender labels and gender identities, including 'non-binary', 'genderqueer', 'genderfluid', 'gendervariant'; they may live as women, men, neither, and/or both, again according to choice and to situation.

There is an increased visibility in transpeople thanks to both legal recognition of gender identity as a protected characteristic in a number of countries and because of the availability of medical interventions to allow a person to change gender physically. Therefore, theologies grounded in the experience of trans lives are relatively recent. Within queer theologies, the focus on trans lives destabilises traditional binary ideas of gender. Concern from conservative Christians often points to the physicality of a transperson, exploring biology and surgical procedures, while transpeople themselves focus on the question of identity. There are a number of texts which have emerged in which trans Christians speak for themselves, including *Transgendering Faith: Identity, Spirituality and*

Sexuality (Dresser, 2004), *Trans/formations* (Althaus-Reid & Isherwood, 2009), *This is My Body: Hearing the Theology of Transgender Christians* (Beardsley & O'Brien, 2016) and *Transfaith* (Dowd, Beardsley & Tanis, 2018).

One significant text on transgender theology and ministry is Justin Tanis's *Trans Gendered: Theology, Ministries and Communities of Faith* (Tanis, 2018). Writing as a trans person on trans issues, Tanis explores a range of topics grounded in the real-life experiences of trans people, offering his own life-story narrative and including sections on a search for selfhood and gender variance in the scriptures. Within the volume, Tanis explores the experience of trans people in their faith communities as well as offering guidance for communities of faith that seek to welcome trans people authentically. In the chapter on 'transgendered theological thought', Tanis explores concepts relating to how gender is beyond male and female and how gender is a calling from God. Tanis's work is seen as ground-breaking scholarship in the area of trans theologies.

In *Transgendering Faith: Identity, Spirituality and Sexuality* (Dresser, 2004), one of the voices we hear describes the difficulties faced following the decision to transition. Dzintra Alksnitis talks about the gifts received from the Holy Spirit during the most challenging and scary period of their life: 'The gifts I received as I had cried out to the Spirit were peace, understanding, love, courage, faith, and wisdom. Little did I know that I was going to need every one of these in order to survive and grow' (Alksnitis, 2004: 31). Elsewhere, Terry Dresser describes their transition from female to male and how they grew to hate their body and began self-mutilation as breasts developed on their body during puberty. This also resulted in a rejection from church. However, the difficult journey results in self-acceptance; as they say, 'I've been lucky to have a close relationship with God and to know deep down inside that no matter what others said I knew God loved me and accepted me as the child God created me to be' (Dresser, 2004: 42).

The spirit of queer theologies – its subversive nature, its danger and playfulness – is brilliantly described in an episode in the life of Siân Taylder, a Catholic transwoman in *Trans/formations* (Althaus-Reid & Isherwood, 2009). Taylder experienced employment discrimination in El Salvador at a Catholic institute where she had applied for a post. She was told her personal circumstances (being trans) were not compatible with the ethos of the school. Taylder brushes this off, stating 'I, in turn, practise a rigid system of discrimination against those who subscribe to racist, homophobic (transphobic?) or sexist points of view. It's a theology of *quid pro quo*, and I don't see why I should be expected to tolerate those who refuse to tolerate me' (2009: 72). Taylder later returns to the church next to the school during the celebration of Sunday Mass and looks her discriminators in the eyes. For Taylder, queer theologies are 'a gloriously inappropriate clash of the decent and the indecent' (2009: 73). She asks, 'You think my theology's a little too aggressive?' (2009: 73). Clashes and conflict with conservative theologies are unavoidable in queer theologies.

It is important to engage with trans Christians when producing trans theologies, so that they are grounded in real-life experiences rather than being speculative or generalised. The production of trans theologies without engagement with trans communities is a concern of Mercia McMahon. She notices the limitations of trans theologies produced by non-trans people and states how this situation is unavoidable, given the low number of trans theologians. To ensure trans voices are included in theologies, she calls for a commitment to working with trans communities; as she says:

> The ideal trans theology is one that is written by members of trans communities, but with so few trans identified theologians this is a long way from becoming reality. Due to this situation those who engage in trans positive theology as outsiders need to be careful that they are fully engaging with the community and not making assumptions about what trans people experience (McMahon, 2016: 61).

THEOLOGIES OF INTERSEX LIVES

Intersex is used to describe an individual whose physical sex or reproductive anatomy do not align to typical definitions of female or male. Hormones and genitalia in intersex people are various. Biologically, chromosomes attributed to a male are XY and to a female XX, so they exist in a binary. In intersex people there are multiple combinations and variations, such as XX, XY, XXY, XX/XY. In many cases, intersex is not identifiable at birth and sometimes it only becomes identifiable during puberty. People with intersex bodies may only be diagnosed during adulthood when there may be problems with fertility, for example. Many intersex people go undiagnosed throughout their lives. There has been a clinical term, 'Disorder in Sex Development' (or DSD for short), but the use of this term, specifically the word 'disorder', is considered unhelpful despite its usage in medicine. It is more appropriate to talk about intersex bodies. Even more controversial is the use of surgical interventions on babies to attempt to align external genitalia cosmetically to male or female. Intersex activists challenge such interventions as they are harmful and the young person cannot consent.

Susannah Cornwall is a pioneer in the field of intersex bodies and Christian theology, undertaking the first full-length examination of intersex bodies and theology in her book entitled *Sex and Uncertainty in the Body of Christ* (Cornwall, 2010). The book explores intersex bodies in relation to medical interventions and theological perspectives, including the themes of incarnation and the Body of Christ. Cornwall's publications in this area are extensive. In placing value on the theologies from intersex lives, Cornwall highlights the importance and value in listening to the theological insights from intersex people:

> Intersex people have their own stories to tell, and ... the Church needs to listen. If the memory and story of Jesus are embodied by those who share in it, then the body of Christ is also an intersex body, constituted and subverted by those intersex Christians whose lives are testimonies of the place faith has held in their journeys (Cornwall, 2014: 31).

Cornwall's interviews with ten intersex-identifying people demonstrate a common feeling among her participants that they are made as God intended (Cornwall, 2013). Some participants see their intersex bodies as unique, bringing spiritual gifts. One participant feels this gift gives her the impetus to educate people more about intersex. These accounts reveal how intersex people put their faith, and relationship with God, above other sources of authority such as the Bible or church.

In *Undoing Theology* (Greenough, 2018), Alyce tells her story as an intersex Christian. Assigned male at birth and brought up to present as male throughout her life, Alyce shares her experience at the age of 62, where she is coming to terms with her undiagnosed intersex body. She describes herself as XXY Catholic. Her story narrates the childhood trauma described through internal feelings of sin and shame, thorough adolescent anguish and episodes of bullying. There is a conflict in her presentation, as an assigned male who feels female. Nevertheless, theologically Alyce sees how her body is made in the image of God; as she states:

> As far as God's gender, I was taught that I was made in His image and likeness. Therefore, God is just like me. Of course, everyone can make the same claim. But the bottom line is that God made me as I am, and I must accept that and thank Him. I'm working on it (Greenough, 2018: 92).

ASEXUALITY/CELIBACY

Asexual people do not experience sexual attraction to others. There are a number of related terms. The term used as the opposite of asexual, that's to say those who experience sexual attraction, is allosexual. Aromantic people experience little or no romantic attraction to others. To be grey-asexual means that sexual attraction is sometimes experienced. An individual identifying as demi-sexual experiences a personal and emotional connection with someone before sexual attraction. Also, the term autosexual has come into usage to denote someone who is attracted to themselves or sexually active with themselves.

Asexuality disturbs or queers the expectation that people will relate to one another sexually. In terms of theologies of sexuality, Elizabeth Stuart points out a general absence of asexual voices in theology, stating how 'asexual people are currently an almost completely silenced group within the theology of sexuality [...] and the asexual person should raise uncomfortable questions for all of us who have valorised sex and sexual desire perhaps at the expense of relationship' (Stuart, 2014: 29). In the Hebrew Bible/Old Testament there are numerous references which point to the goodness of sexual relations, especially in terms of reproduction. In Genesis 9:7 we see how God/Yahweh says to Noah, 'as for you, be fruitful and increase in number; multiply on the earth and increase upon it'.

Celibacy describes a commitment to refraining from sexual activity. Within Christianity the promotion of celibacy as ideal has resulted in language such as virginity, purity, and chastity being used to promote sexual abstinence. Celibacy is also promoted by the churches, as we have seen above, as the path people who feel same-sex attraction must take. It is also a requirement within Catholicism for those who undertake religious orders, as giving up sex is considered to enhance a religious person's spiritual gifts. Within the New Testament we see how celibacy is promoted as an ideal state for Christians, particularly in the letters of Paul. In one example, 1 Corinthians 7, Paul does not say that it is wrong to get married, but that it is better for Christians to stay single. Paul puts forward that being married means a man has to focus on his wife, while being single means he can focus on the Lord's work. He states: 'I wish that all of you were [single] as I am. But each of you has your own gift from God; one has this gift, another has that.' Paul's preference for celibacy is traditionally seen as a concession rather than a command. Nonetheless, this and other scriptures are interpreted to promote celibacy as part of spiritual discernment among those who have taken holy orders.

The 'ex-gay' movement is a Christian-organised drive to discourage people from same-sex activity. Based on the idea of conversion therapy, it views same-sex desires as ungodly and sinful. Being gay is incompatible with being Christian in the movement. It considers that people can 'convert' from having same-sex desires to being heterosexual. The 'ex-gay' movement was a popular practice in evangelical circles in the USA. During the process of 'conversion', gay-identifying people should ignore their sexuality and attempt to change it. Therefore, the gay, lesbian or bisexual person commits to celibacy or heterosexuality. The full conversion is often seen as complete when an 'ex-gay' individual commits to heterosexual marriage. The movement was damning and caused intense psychological and emotional damage to the gay-identifying people who underwent the therapy. Gay conversion therapy is widely acknowledged as connected to the risk of self-harm and suicide. Those who survived the intense psychological damage caused by the 'ex-gay' movement and the attempt at conversion therapy are known as 'ex-gay survivors'.

STRAIGHT QUEERS

Can a straight identified person do queer theologies? There is an assumption that to engage with queer theologies or queer biblical studies a person has to be LGBTQ+ in some way. Deryn Guest queries how there may be some justification for writing from the space of one's identity, stating how those 'who choose to self-identify as such, have experiences of looking that derive from that' (Guest, 2012: 152). Guest concludes that heterosexual-identifying people who engage with queer projects 'step aside from, or deliberately disinherit themselves from, the more normative and privileged aspects of their identities' (2012: 159). So, to identify as 'queer' involves a sacrifice of the social privilege which comes with heteronormativity.

Queer disrupts binaries and destabilises identity and authority. An individual does not need a particular set of credentials or to self-identify in a certain way to engage in the task of queering theology. As queer theologies disrupt and interrogate traditional theology, the task of queering theology is one which can include heterosexual or 'straight' people. Althaus-Reid puts it very simply: 'let us remember here that the Genderfucker may also be straight' (Althaus-Reid, 2003: 68). The principle for inclusion is a commitment to justice. Heterosexual queers may be allies to LGBTQ+ people. In this vein, Kwok Pui-lan asserts:

> Sexual theology is not just the specific concern of queer, gay, lesbian, bisexual and transgendered theologians – as it is often assumed to be – but a project that all theologians, whether consciously or unconsciously, participate in (Kwok, 2003: 151).

Cornwall is an example of a self-identifying cisgender, heterosexual woman who has excelled in the field of queer theologies. Cornwall describes herself and her work as 'a non-intersex person who writes about intersex; as a cisgender person who writes about transgender; as an able person who writes about disability; as a straight married person who writes about queer theology' (Cornwall, 2017: 41). She moves beyond categories of identification to highlight the agenda for justice within her work:

> Queer theory, queer theology and queer biblical criticism are increasingly taught in universities and seminaries as postmodern methodologies alongside a range of others, often by scholars who do not call themselves queer. I am one such scholar. I am a heterosexual married cisgender woman, and I do not claim anything very subversive about me or my life. I try to bring into question unjust sexual, gender and economic relations, and to model respectful pedagogies and dynamics with my students (Cornwall, 2017: 32).

Of course, Cornwall herself acknowledges that writing from one's position as LGBTQ+ can offer further insights for queer theologies. She states how 'transgender people know things about transgender experience that I do not: of course, that is indubitably true' (Cornwall, 2017: 41). In one example of the commitment to just sexual, gender, and economic relations, Cornwall claims that transgender experience is also human experience and is therefore something all human beings should take an interest in.

Self-disclosure is an important element to offering one's position in the production of queer theologies. Queer theologians and those working at the intersections of gender, sexuality, race, class, dis/ability, and other positions that inform their writing usually reveal their own self-identifications and positions and how these influence their work. This allows for transparency and demonstrates how the author is aware that their own positional influence may shape, or limit, their work.

KINKY CHRISTIANS

The acronym BDSM is used to represent the practice of bondage, discipline/dominance, submission/sadism, masochism. It is the practice of role-playing and of inflicting pain or receiving pain, depending on whether a participant is dominant or submissive. For those who practise it, engaging in BDSM is often seen as pleasurable, satisfying, and even healing. Within contemporary culture the practice has become popularised through literature and film, such as *50 Shades of Grey* (James, 2011) and the sequels. In sociology and psychology, studies about the participants and acts of BDSM practices helps us to understand elements of human desire: how and why we relate to one another, and about our own needs. On a cultural level, the idea of BDSM is broadly connected to Christian religious imagery, including crucifixes, crowns of thorns, whips. Christianity has a long history of self-inflicted pain; from those who took religious orders who discipline themselves through flogging, to the wearing of chastity belts or other torturous instruments to regulate personal sexual desire.

In feminist theology, Mary Daly's *Gyn/Ecology* (1978) describes the 'sadomasochistic gospel that proclaims that female suffering is joy' (Daly, 1978: 93–94). Daly goes on to offer an example of such narratives, including Mary's pregnancy by the Holy Ghost and the torturous scene of the crucifixion. She says how 'torture for "higher causes", religious and secular, has always been legitimised by christian cross-bearers' [*sic*] (1978: 95). It is not too difficult to see how the Christian narrative is connected to ideas of dominance and submission; it is a narrative that has pain and suffering at its core in the crucifixion of Jesus. Daly relates the idea of control and pain to patriarchy.

In BDSM, the person who is dominant is called a 'top' and the submissive partner is 'bottom'. Althaus-Reid relocates the idea of sadomasochism and applies it to the struggle for liberation in Latin America. Althaus-Reid describes God as the 'top' and the Christian as the 'bottom'. She calls this a 'master sketch of Christianity done in a moment' (Althaus-Reid, 2000: 153). Yet she highlights a significant difference, that 'the desire for a whip in a fetish scenario is not the same as experiencing the whip of the God the Father' (2000: 153). The Father's whip is too close to the dominant ideas of political repression of the poor. The difference Althaus-Reid highlights is that of consent. In a BDSM scene, the bottom and top negotiate the act beforehand, they consent, and there is usually a code, known as a 'safeword', which may be called as an instruction to stop. The dynamics of top and bottom do not simply show control of the top to the bottom, as the top largely carries out the wishes of the bottom as negotiated beforehand. In an analogy not too far away from Christianity, this negotiated space could be similar to prayer.

A theology of BDSM becomes a source for queer theologies, as it disrupts the sexual codes cherished by Christianity. Sex between a man and woman designated for procreation is turned upside down when the scene is about pain and pleasure. A theology of BDSM is not necessarily about gender or sexuality, as the practice may or may not involve genitals. It is therefore not unusual for same-sex partners to play together, even where one or both are heterosexual. One detailed account of the theological considerations of a Christian who engages in kink practices is located in the story of Cath, a Christian who engages in BDSM (Greenough, 2018). For Cath, the practice allows her to gain spiritual and emotional freedom. As she engages in rope play through being tied up, she experiences a meditative state which allows her to focus and simply to be. This allows Cath to meditate on God, and she describes how she finds the process healing. She says, 'the act of being spanked or flogged or cropped or such like gives me permission to cry out. It's a safe way of letting all these emotions out, without fear of being judged for them. A sort of cathartic release. Very often I'm left feeling very peaceful afterwards' (2018: 144).

A discussion of BDSM and Christianity is taboo for many, and some readers of stories and theologies connected to kink activity may feel a little uncomfortable. Queer theologies are about rupture, disturbing, so the feeling of discomfort is actually part of the project.

QUEER NUNS: SISTERS OF PERPETUAL INDULGENCE

The Sisters of Perpetual Indulgence (SPI) is an order of drag nuns committed to protest and social justice for LGBTQ+ people. There are orders in the USA, UK, Europe, Canada, Australia, and Latin America. The nuns have a variety of gender and sexual identities, but the majority are gay men. In dragging up as Catholic nuns they often retain gendered features such as beards, but with heavy makeup applied. The Sisters are an activist organisation, fundraising for charities, especially for HIV/AIDS and cancer care. They are committed to raising awareness of sexual health, and dedicated to the eradication of homophobia, racism, classism, and other prejudiced-based behaviours. They offer outreach and support.

Queer Nuns: Religion, Activism and Serious Parody (Wilcox, 2018) provides an in-depth examination of the Sisters of Perpetual Indulgence. Wilcox traces the origins of the first San Francisco order (in

1979) and its spread across the globe: Canada (1981), Australia (1983), England and France (1990), and Germany (1991). Of course, the Sisters parody the religious nuns of Roman Catholicism in their dress, yet this parody leads to serious activism. Wilcox demonstrates how 'genderfuck meets religionfuck' (Wilcox, 2018: 129), noting how playing with gender presents itself to conservative audiences as 'whores in virgins' clothing, importing psychological and physical illness and the sinful nature of their sex into the purest possible human space' (2018: 137). Presenting as nuns in this way makes queer religious identities visible. It queers religion as it disrupts normative presentations of religion and the human body. Moreover, the identity of nun is one which is dedicated to service. The idea of 'religionfuck' raises important questions over cultural assumptions about religious identities, beliefs, and practices. In claiming their identity as nuns, the Sisters believe the following:

> (1) the Sisters do the same work as nuns do, sometimes they do it better, and they are more fun; (2) they have more moral integrity than the Roman Catholic Church, especially toward queer communities and toward Roman Catholic nuns; (3) their work is spiritual or even prophetic, like that of vowed women religious; and (4) the Roman Catholic Church has no monopoly on nuns anyway (Wilcox, 2018: 88).

The range of religious beliefs and practices among the Sisters varies – from secular Sisters to those who attend Catholic worship. By and large, the majority of the Sisters claim to be spiritual rather than religious, denoting a rejection of the traditional idea of religion with its structures of authority. Often the Sisters blend traditions and beliefs in practising their spirituality. One of the nuns Wilcox interviewed is a former ex-gay man ordained in the Church, known as Sister Krissy Fiction – a parody name on the word 'crucifixion'. Sister Krissy describes herself as a 'spiritual slut' (Wilcox, 2018: 190). Sister Krissy uses a metaphor of religions as language. She adds, 'so I say I'm fluent in Christianity and fluent in neopaganism, I can kind of ask where the bathroom is in Buddhism' (2018: 191). One of the nuns who is Catholic talks about how her ministry in raising awareness of the importance of sexual health is inspired by Jesus. Sister Marie says:

I look at the example of Jesus, I see that work of accepting people where they are, no matter what. Instead of jumping on the woman caught in adultery, saying, 'Well go and do better. Go do better next time' ... We're trying to do the same thing. 'Here's a condom. Go do better next time. We're here for you' (Wilcox, 2018: 193).

Exploring the work of the Sisters offers a fascinating lens into how religious or spiritual beliefs are queered. They are shown to be performative, unstable structures and this is highlighted through their parody. The dragging up of men as nuns destabilises the idea of solid, firm, religious identities. It demonstrates performative, embodied, and activist living queer theologies.

CONCLUSION

The sharing of life stories from queer Christians can be empowering and transformative. The stories are relational and remind us of the fact that we are not alone. In the opening to her work on lesbian biblical hermeneutics, Guest writes about how she had never met a lesbian, and the word held connotations of undesirable attributes reserved for those who lived unfulfilled, tragic lives. Her mother had handed her a Christian pamphlet on the trials of being a teenager, which warned against developing crushes on the same sex. Despite her mother's intentions, Guest writes, 'I was glad to hear about these women because it was at least a relief to know that there were other women out there who were attracted to members of their own sex' (Guest, 2005: 3). For LGBTQ+ people working through issues of gender or sexuality alongside their Christian faith, reading and learning from others' experience can be a source of strength, hope, and nourishment. This is where queer theologies become practical theologies.

In theological terms, the sharing of stories can also be problematic. The construction of theologies from the vantage point of our gender and sexual identities can result in new theologies deemed indecent, sexual, or taboo. Conservative Christians often dismiss such theologies as indulgent, self-serving, and too far removed from recognisable Christianity. Yet queer theologies expose how Christianity, constructed with blocks of patriarchy and cemented with hetero- and cisnormativity, is a performance, sustained and repeated. Queer lives and those who inhabit Christianity differently break through this.

As this chapter has discussed the importance of listening to the experience of queer Christians, I am sensitive to the numerous voices which have not been included here, or those who are silenced or have yet to speak. Moreover, one voice is not representative of a particular group: the experience of one is not the same as the other. 'Theology' is God-talk, and it must be open to endless conversations from endless voices.

FURTHER READING AND ONLINE RESOURCES

Althaus-Reid, M. and Isherwood, L. (2009) (Eds.) *Trans/formations*. London: SCM Press.

A range of essays discussing trans theologies.

Beardsley, C. and O'Brien, M. (Eds.) (2016) *This is My Body: hearing the theology of transgender Christians*. London: Darton, Longman and Todd.

This book, written by trans people, explores individual trans experiences with faith. It serves to redress the balance to allow those who identify as trans to produce their own theologies.

Cornwall, S. (Ed.) (2015) *Intersex, Theology, and the Bible. Troubling Bodies in Church, Text, and Society*. New York: Palgrave Macmillan.

Insightful discussions looking at intersex from a range of perspectives: life stories, biblical studies, pastoral care.

Greenough, C. (2018) *Undoing Theology: Life Stories from Non-normative Christians*. London: SCM Press.

This book details the advantages and transformative possibilities of exploring life stories as a source for theology, as readers engage with the biographical and spiritual journeys of three non-normative Christians: an intersex Catholic, an ex-gay minister, and a Christian who engages in fetish practices.

Robinson, B. (Ed.) (2017) *Our Witness: The Unheard Stories of LGBT+ Christians*. London: Darton, Longman and Todd.

This book provides powerful stories of LGBT+ Christians and their witness to the churches. The stories look at the experiences of rejection and marginalisation of LGBTQ+ Christians by the churches, but also at how LGBTQ+ Christians reconcile their faith with their gender or sexuality and the gifts this brings.

Tanis, J. (2018) *Trans-Gendered: Theology, Ministry, and Communities of Faith.* Ohio: Pilgrim Press.

A second edition of Tanis's comprehensive consideration of trans theologies, first printed in 2003. Tanis covers a wealth of topics, including trans body theologies and how churches can offer genuine affirmation and welcome to trans people.

Wilcox, M. (2018) *Queer Nuns: Religious Activism and Serious Parody.* New York: New York University Press.

A comprehensive examination of the religious/spiritual lives of the Sisters of Perpetual Indulgence and their commitment to activism for social justice.

www.queergrace.com

An online resource to explore LGBTQ+ lives and Christian faith. The website contains podcasts, videos, documentaries, online resources, stories, and a virtual community.

REFERENCES

Alksnitis, D. (2004) 'Living in the Palm of God' in McCall Tigert, L. and Tirabassi, M. C. (Eds.) *Transgendering Faith: Identity, Spirituality and Sexuality*, pp. 29–30. Ohio: Pilgrim Press.

Althaus-Reid, M. (2000) *Indecent Theology.* London: Routledge.

Althaus-Reid, M. (2003) *The Queer God.* London: Routledge.

Althaus-Reid, M. and Isherwood, L. (Eds.) (2009) *Trans/formations.* London: SCM Press.

Anglican Communion Office (1998 Lambeth Conference, published 2005) 'Lambeth Conference Resolutions Archive Index of Resolutions from 1998'. Available at: https://www.anglicancommunion.org/media/76650/1998.pdf

Beardsley, C. and O'Brien, M. (Eds.) (2016) *This is My Body: hearing the theology of transgender Christians.* London: Darton, Longman and Todd.

Catechism of the Catholic Church (1993) Available at: http://www.vatican.va/archive/ccc_css/archive/catechism/p3s2c2a6.htm

Congregation for Catholic Education (2005) 'Instruction Concerning the Criteria for the Discernment of Vocations with regard to Persons with Homosexual Tendencies in view of their Admission to the Seminary and to Holy Orders'. Available at: http://www.vatican.va/roman_curia/congregations/cca theduc/documents/rc_con_ccatheduc_doc_20051104_istruzione_en.html

Congregation for the Doctrine of the Faith (1986) 'Letter to the Bishops of the Catholic Church on the Pastoral Care of Homosexual Persons'. Available at: http://www.vatican.va/roman_curia/congregations/cfaith/documents/rc_con _cfaith_doc_19861001_homosexual-persons_en.html

Congregation for the Doctrine of the Faith (2003) 'Considerations Regarding Proposals to Give Legal Recognition to Unions between Homosexual Persons'. Available at: http://www.vatican.va/roman_curia/congregations/cfa ith/documents/rc_con_cfaith_doc_20030731_homosexual-unions_en.html

Cornwall, S. (2010) *Sex and Uncertainty in the Body of Christ: Intersex Conditions and Christian Theology*. London: Equinox.

Cornwall, S. (2013) British Intersex Christians. Accounts of Intersex Identity, Christian Identity and Church Experience. *Practical Theology*, 6(2), pp. 220–236.

Cornwall, S. (2014) Telling Stories about Intersex and Christianity: Saying Too Much or Not Saying Enough? *Theology*, 117(1), pp. 24–33.

Cornwall, S. (2017) Home and hiddenness: queer theology, domestication and institutions. *Theology & Sexuality*, 23(1–2), pp. 31–47.

Daly, M. (1978) *Gyn/Ecology. The Metaethics of Radical Feminism*. Boston: Beacon Press.

Dickinson, C. and Toomey, M. (2017) The continuing relevance of 'queer' theology for the rest of the field. *Theology & Sexuality*, 23(1–2), pp. 1–16.

Dowd, C., Beardsley, C. and Tanis, J. (2018) *Transfaith*. London: Darton, Longman and Todd.

Dresser, T. (2004) 'Terry's Journey', in McCall Tigert, L. and Tirabassi, M. C. (Eds.) *Transgendering Faith: Identity, Spirituality and Sexuality*, pp. 40–42. Ohio: Pilgrim Press.

Ford, M. (2004) *Disclosures: Conversions Gay and Spiritual*. London: Darton, Longman and Todd.

Greenough, C. (2018) *Undoing Theology: Life Stories from Non-normative Christians*. London: SCM Press.

Guest, D. (2005) *When Deborah Met Jael: Lesbian Biblical Hermeneutics*. London: SCM Press.

Guest, D. (2012) *Beyond Feminist Biblical Studies*. Sheffield: Sheffield University Press.

House of Bishops (2003) *Some Issues in Human Sexuality: A Guide to the Debate*. London: Church House Publishing.

James, E. L. (2011) *Fifty Shades of Grey*. London: Arrow.

Kwok, P-L. (2003) Theology as a Sexual Act? *Feminist Theology*, 11(2), pp. 149–156.

Larrimore, M. (2015) 'Introduction', in Talvacchia, K. T., Pettinger, M. F. and Larrimore, M. (Eds.) *Queer Christianities. Lived Religion in Transgressive Forms*, pp. 1–10. New York: New York University Press.

McCall Tigert, L. and Tirabassi, M. C. (Eds.) (2004) *Transgendering Faith: Identity, Spirituality and Sexuality*. Ohio: Pilgrim Press.

McMahon, M. (2016) 'Trans Liberating Feminist and Queer Theologies', in Beardsley, C. and O'Brien, M. (Eds.) *This is My Body. Hearing the Theology of Transgender Christians*, pp. 59–60. London: Darton, Longman and Todd.

Nixon, D. (2008) No More Tea, Vicar: An Exploration of the Discourses which Inform the Current Debates about Sexualities within the Church of England. *Sexualities*, 11, pp. 595–620.

Stuart, E. (2014) 'The Theological Study of Sexuality', in Thatcher, A. (Ed.) *The Oxford Handbook of Theology, Sexuality and Gender*, pp. 18–31. Oxford: Oxford University Press.

Tanis, J. (2018) *Trans-Gendered: Theology, Ministry, and Communities of Faith*. Ohio: Pilgrim Press.

Taylder, S. (2009) 'Shot from both Sides: Theology and the Woman Who Isn't Quite What She Seems', in Althaus-Reid, M. and Isherwood, L. (Eds.) *Trans/formations*, pp. 70–91. London: SCM Press.

Toft, A. (2009) 'Bisexual Christians', in Hunt, S. (Ed.) *Contemporary Christianities and LGBT Sexualities*, pp. 67–86. Surrey: Ashgate.

Toft, A. (2014) Re-imagining bisexuality and Christianity: The negotiation of Christianity in the lives of bisexual women and men, *Sexualities*, 17(5–6), pp. 546–564.

Wilcox, M. (2002) When Sheila's a Lesbian: Religious Individualism among Lesbian, Gay, Bisexual, and Transgender Christians. *Sociology of Religion*, 63 (4), pp. 497–513.

Wilcox, M. (2003) *Coming Out in Christianity: Religion, Identity and Community*. Bloomington: Indiana University Press.

Wilcox, M. (2009) *Queer Women and Religious Individualism*. Bloomington: Indiana University Press.

Wilcox, M. (2018) *Queer Nuns: Religious Activism and Serious Parody*. New York: New York University Press.

Yip, A. K. T. (1997) *Gay Male Christian Couples: Life Stories*. Westport, CT: Praeger.

Yip, A. K. T. (2000) 'Leaving the church to keep my faith: the lived experiences of non-heterosexual Christians', in Francis, L. J. and Katz, Y. J. (Eds.) *Joining and Leaving Religion: Research Perspectives*, pp. 129–145. Leominster: Gracewing.

Yip, A. K. T. (2002) The Persistence of Faith Among Non-Heterosexual Christians: Evidence for the Neosecularization Thesis of Religious Transformation. *Journal for the Scientific Study of Religion*, 41(2), pp. 199–212.

Yip, A. K. T. (2003) Spirituality and Sexuality: An Exploration of the Religious Beliefs of Non-Heterosexual Christians in Great Britain. *Theology & Sexuality* 9(2), pp. 137–154.

Yip, A. K. T. (2010) 'Coming Home from the Wilderness: An Overview of Recent Scholarly Research on LGBTQI Religiosity/Spirituality', in Browne, K., Munt, S. R. and Yip, A. K. T. (Eds.) *Queer Spiritual Spaces: Sexuality and Sacred Places*, pp. 35–50. Farnham: Ashgate.

AFTERWORD: BEYOND THE BASICS

> Queer theology throws open the shutters, allowing the sun to stream in, and showing up just how dusty and threadbare some of those theological rugs really are (Cornwall, 2011: 252).

Some dusty and threadbare theological rugs are cherished as heirlooms, handed down with sentimentality having served a purpose for Christian thought throughout the ages. What is trash to one person is treasure to another. This means that there are tensions between queer theologies and mainstream theologies. Deryn Guest describes queer as 'the critical undo-er ... an approach that squatted everywhere but refused to be defined or packaged, it managed to upset everyone' (Guest, 2012: 43). Within queer theologies the upset extends beyond the academy, as Church and State hold stakes in theological conversations. Public institutions are interwoven with long histories of religious influence. While queer theologies resist and interrogate mainstream theologies, mainstream theologies may resist the queer project. Sara Ahmed notes how, 'when we speak about what we come up against, we come up against what we speak about. Another way of saying: walls come up when we talk about walls' (Ahmed, 2017: 148).

Christian theology is over 2,000 years old, yet queer Christian theologies are still breaking their teeth, as queer theory was first coined by Teresa de Lauretis in 1990. Within the academy there is much rich intellectual attention given to queer theologies; the basics of such work are presented throughout the pages of this book. Within the churches there are ongoing heated and muddled conversations around the issues of LGBTQ+ inclusion. Within society there are debates and repercussions for those who subvert normative gender and sexualities, and this is further compacted in contexts where legislative measures do not exist in order to protect individual characteristics. Even in countries with such legal positions, prejudice and discrimination still exist. Gender, sexual orientation, and religion are intersectional characteristics but sometimes they collide. In the public sphere we see this in media reports of business people who refuse to serve same-sex couples, grounding their refusal in their religious beliefs. Where there are tensions, there is still much work to be done. The triad of academy, Church, and State mean that queer theologies disrupt different systems and are taken up in different ways. Whether they are considered self-indulgent, too personal, too intellectual or too theoretical, future queer theologies must pay attention to Isherwood and Althaus-Reid's injunction that 'queering theology is not a rhetorical pastime but a political duty' (Isherwood & Althaus-Reid, 2004: 3). Or, as Jeff Hood states, 'theology without the practical is dead, and dead theologies do not bring about the resurrection. I seek theology that speaks life into death' (Hood, 2015: 1).

Queer theologies disrupt the stability of identity and tackle the power structures at play in identity construction. Queer has also been used as a catch-all collective term for LGBTQ+ identities, although as a theory it was never intended to function in this way. Given these two functions – disruption of identities and critical analysis of theology in light of identities – queer theologies are always plural. They speak in different languages and cover a range of issues and methods. Queer theologies do not even agree with one another. One of the delights in researching this area of study is to explore the range of topics and approaches on offer.

In suggesting helpful ways for the motivated reader to move beyond the basics, the first task is to engage in the suggested reading and resources in each chapter, as well as the reference texts. To offer one important reminder: these texts can be challenging and complex, offering ideas which delight and confuse within the pages. In addition to those extensive references, I offer the following recent publications as suggested reading for those seeking to go beyond the basics presented in this book. Three emerging major themes covered in these texts include queer eco-theologies, the application of queer theory, and queer theologies' concern with capitalism.

FURTHER READING

Bauman, W. A. (Ed.) (2018) Meaningful Flesh. Reflections on Religion and Nature for a Queer Planet. Brooklyn: Punctum Books.

The areas of queer theologies and eco-theologies are successfully combined in this book, which explores the relationship between religion, nature, and queer theory.

Brintnall, K. L., Marchal, J. A. and Moore, S. D. (Eds.) (2018) Sexual Disorientations: Queer Temporalities, Affects, Theologies. New York: Fordham University Press.

The authors of this volume are concerned with how queer theory has not always been applied to the study of theology, and the essays within this collection seek to address this. This is an advanced text, tackling major themes in queer theory, such as queer temporalities and queer affects. The commitment to queer theory means the volume explores new and innovative terrains in queer theologies.

Tonstad, L. (2018) Queer Theology. Beyond Apologetics. Eugene: Wipf and Stock.

In suggesting that queer theologies move beyond apologetic strategies, Tonstad analyses the dynamics between theology, sex, and the economy, revealing how queer theologies are a response to the injustices brought about by capitalism and colonialism. The concluding chapter, 'Queer Theologies to Come', is very helpful in signposting further reading.

REFERENCES

Ahmed, S. (2017) *Living A Feminist Life*. Durham, NC: Duke University Press.
Isherwood, L. (Eds.) *The Sexual Theologian*, pp. 1–15. London: Continuum.
Isherwood, L and Althaus-Reid, M. (2004) 'Queering Theology', in Althaus-Reid, M. and Isherwood, L. (Eds.) *The Sexual Theologian*, pp.1–15. London: Continuum.
Cornwall, S. (2011) *Controversies in Queer Theology*. London: SCM Press.
Guest, D. (2012) *Beyond Feminist Biblical Studies*. Sheffield: Sheffield Phoenix Press.
Hood, J. (2015) *The Courage to Be Queer*. Eugene: Wipf and Stock.

GLOSSARY

ABSTINENCE	The act of restraining oneself from something, including sex.
AGENDER	A person who self-identifies as without a gender identity.
ALLOSEXUAL	Someone who experiences sexual attraction; the opposite of asexual.
ALLY	A person who supports another. This may be a heterosexual person supporting the LGBTQ+ community.
ANGLICAN COMMUNION	A group of worldwide churches historically based on the Church of England.
ANOINTING OF THE SICK	A sacrament in the Roman Catholic Church to bless the sick.
APOLOGETICS	The defence of Christian religious doctrine through reasoned arguments.
AROMANTIC	A person who experiences little or no romantic attraction to others.
ASEXUALITY	A lack of sexual attraction to others.
AUTOSEXUAL	An individual who is sexually aroused by their own body.
BAPTISM	A rite of admission to the Christian Church, through sprinkling of water or full immersion in water.
BDSM	Bondage, discipline/dominance, submission/sadism, masochism.
BIBLIOLATRY	Worship of the Bible.

BIGENDER	A person who experiences two gender identities and may live between the two.
BINARY	Two opposites.
BISEXUALITY	Experience of sexual attraction to more than one gender.
BODY OF CHRIST	Two definitions in Christianity. (i) Jesus's words at the Last Supper: 'This is my body,' in Luke 22:19–20; (ii) used to refer to the Christian Church.
CAMINATA	A walk (Spanish). Based on the theology of Marcella Althaus-Reid, this is the act of practical theology, of walking with one's community.
CAPITALISM	An economic system of private ownership used to generate profits.
CATHOLIC CHURCH	Branch of the Christian Church which accepts the Pope as its leader and is based in Rome.
CELIBACY	Abstaining from sexual relations.
CHASTITY	Refraining from sexual relations.
CHICANA	A girl or woman of Mexican origin and descent.
CHRISTOLOGY	The study of the person, nature, and role of Christ in Christian theology.
COMING OUT	A metaphor relating to the self-disclosure of one's sexual orientation or gender identity.
CONFIRMATION	The rite in which a baptised person affirms their Christian belief as a full member of the Church.
CONSENT	To give permission; to authorise.
CRUISING	To search for a sexual partner.
DECONSTRUCTION	A method of critical analysis of a text in order to show there is no fixed meaning but that it can be understood in a different way by each reader
DEMISEXUAL	Considered half-way between sexual and asexual; a person who does not

	feel a sexual connection without an emotional connection.
DIASPORA	A group of people who spread from one original country to others.
DOCTRINAL	Concerned with a set of beliefs traditionally held and taught by the Church.
DOGMATIC	A system of principles/beliefs set out as undeniably true.
ECCLESIOLOGY	The study of the nature and structure of the churches in Christian theology.
EUCHARIST	A sacrament commemorating the Last Supper in Christian services.
EUNUCH	Generally used in ancient times to denote a man who has been castrated.
EUROCENTRIC	Focused on European culture, history or philosophy.
EX-GAY	A term used to describe someone who has undergone conversion therapy in an attempt to change sexual orientation from being homosexual to heterosexual.
FEMINISM	The advocacy of women's rights, examining how inequalities between men and women should be challenged.
FIRST-WAVE FEMINISM	A period of feminist activity in the 19th and early 20th centuries which focused on legal rights for women, particularly the right to vote.
GENDER-FLUID	A person who does not relate to a specific gender.
GENDERQUEER	A person who does not identify with a particular gender but may identify as neither male nor female, both, or a combination of binary gender.
GREY-ASEXUAL	Between sexuality and asexuality; someone identifying as grey-asexual

	may only experience sexual attraction occasionally.
HEGEMONY	Leadership or dominance of one social group over another.
HERMENEUTICS	The area of study that deals with interpretation of the Bible.
HETERONORMATIVITY	The idea that heterosexuality is the normal sexual orientation.
HETEROSEXISM	Discrimination against homosexuality on the grounds that one considers heterosexuality to be the normal sexual orientation.
HETEROSEXUALITY	Attraction to the opposite sex.
HETERO-SUSPICION	A method of removing the presumption that all people are heterosexual; being suspicious of gender.
HISTORICAL-CRITICISM	The study of the world and origins of ancient texts.
HOLY ORDERS	A rite of passage to religious orders; ordination as a member of the clergy.
HOMOSEXUALITY	Sexual attraction to people of the same sex.
INCARNATION	When a deity takes human form. In Christian theology, the person of Jesus Christ, God as human incarnate.
INTERSECTIONALITY	A framework that shows how systems of oppression and discrimination are multiple. The most marginalised people therefore fall under multiple minority groups.
INTERSEX	A person whose sex does not align with traditional biological expectations of male or female.
JUBILEES	An event celebrated by African American communities to mark the end of slavery, based on Leviticus 25:9–10.
KINKY	Unusual sexual behaviour.

LATINX	A non-binary term to refer to a person of Latin American origin, used instead of latino/latina.
LGBTQ+	Lesbian, gay, bisexual, trans, and queer (+ other non-normative expressions of gender and identity).
LITERARY CRITICISM	In religious studies, the practice of viewing the Bible as a suitable object for literary study rather than as an exclusively sacred text.
LITURGY	A particular form of worship.
MESTIZA	In Latin America, a woman of mixed race.
MISOGYNY	Dislike or contempt for women.
MONOGAMY	Being married to or having a relationship with one person at a time.
MONOLITHIC	Something that is large, united, and difficult to change.
MUJERISTA	Concerned with Hispanic women's liberation and feminism.
NON-BINARY	Someone whose gender identity is neither male nor female.
NON-NORMATIVE	Not conforming to normative expectations of gender and/or sexuality.
NORMATIVITY	Relating to a standard expectation of gender/sexuality.
PAGANISM	Range of spiritual beliefs and practices, including nature worship, different from those in main world religions.
PANSEXUALITY	A form of sexuality where preference is not limited by gender identity.
PATRIARCHY	A society or community in which men hold power and women are largely excluded.
PNEUMATOLOGY	The study of the Holy Spirit in Christian theology.
POLARI	A form of slang, formerly used by gay people.

POLYSEXUALITY | Sexual attraction to more than one gender.

POST-CHRISTIAN | Someone who chooses to distance themselves from the language and assumptions of traditional Christianity, including sexism.

POSTCOLONIALISM | The study or examination of the lasting impact of colonialism, including the cultural legacy of control and exploitation.

POSTMODERNISM | The theory that there is no absolute truth, that in the postmodern world everything is shaped by the cultural context of a particular time and place and community.

POST-STRUCTURALISM | A critical theory that rejects framework and structure as methods of analysis.

PROFEMINIST | A commitment to challenge sexism and gender injustice; someone in favour of supporting feminism.

PURITY | The state of considering not having sex as morally good.

QUEER | (i) (verb) to disturb, disrupt, spoil or ruin; (ii) (noun) someone who is non-normative.

QUEER THEORY | A critical theory which works to disrupt normative ways of thinking.

QUESTIONING | Someone who is questioning their sexual identity.

RECEPTION CRITICISM (READER-RESPONSE) | How a text, such as the Bible, has been received by the reader and how their position informs their reading of the text.

RECLAMATION | The act of claiming something back.

RECONCILIATION | A sacrament in Roman Catholicism where an individual acknowledges their sins to a priest and are absolved of them.

RE-ENGAGEMENT	An act of engaging with something again.
RESISTANCE	The refusal to accept or comply with something.
RUPTURE	The act of breaking away from something.
SECOND-WAVE FEMINISM	A period of feminist activities from the 1960s which lasted approximately two decades, including activist activity relating to the workplace, sexuality, and reproductive rights for women.
SLAVE SPIRITUALS	A Christian song which describes the hard and difficult oppressions experienced under slavery.
STRAIGHT	Heterosexual.
SYSTEMATIC THEOLOGY	In theology, systematic theology formulates ordered and reasoned accounts of Christian doctrines, looking at what the Bible teaches or what is known and true about God.
TRANS/TRANSGENDER	A person whose gender identity does not correspond to their sex assigned at birth.
TRANSMAN	Someone who was assigned female at birth but transitions to live as a man.
TRANSSEXUAL	A person who feels they belong to the sex opposite to the one assigned to them at birth, usually seeking medical interventions for physical transitions.
TRANSWOMAN	Someone assigned male at birth but transitions to live as a woman.
VIRGINITY	The state of never having experienced sexual intercourse.
WESTERN	Relating to the countries of Europe and North America.
WOMANIST	A feminist of colour.
ZE, ZIR/HIR, ZIRSELF	Gender-neutral pronouns to replace 'he/she, his/her, himself/herself'.

BIBLICAL REFERENCES INDEX

SUBJECT AND AUTHOR INDEX